CONTENTS

Contents

EVALUATING EDUCATIONAL SOFTWARE

Derek Blease

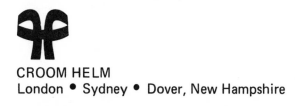

CROOM HELM
London • Sydney • Dover, New Hampshire

© 1986 Derek Blease
Croom Helm Ltd, Provident House, Burrell Row,
Beckenham, Kent BR3 1AT

Croom Helm Australia Pty Ltd, Suite 4, 6th Floor,
64-76 Kippax Street, Surry Hills, NSW 2010, Australia

British Library Cataloguing in Publication Data

Blease, Derek
    Evaluating educational software
    1. Education – Data processing
    2. Microcomputers – Programming
    I. Title
    370'.28'5536   LB1028.43

    ISBN 0-7099-3915-9

Croom Helm, 51 Washington Street, Dover,
New Hampshire 03820, USA

Library of Congress Cataloging-in-Publication Data

Blease, Derek, 1943–
    Evaluating educational software.

    Bibliography: p.137
    Includes index.
    1. Computer-assisted instruction. 2. Computer
literacy. 3. Education, elementary—curricula—
computer programs—evaluation. 4. Education, secondary
—curricula—computer programs—evaluation. I. Title.
LB1028.5.B56   1986   371.3'9445   86-6335
ISBN 0-7099-3915-9

Printed and bound in Great Britain
by Billing & Sons Limited, Worcester.

Contents

PREFACE

The purpose of this book is to help make it easier for
practising teachers and students of education to differentiate
between potentially good software and the rest. However, it is
hoped that teachers who have some programming expertise, and
who are keen to have a go at writing programs for classroom
use, will find the advice contained in this book helpful when
thinking about program design.

The text is aimed at computer users, not computer experts,
and it seeks to stress that a knowledge of computer
programming is not a prerequisite of the effective use of the
microcomputer in the classroom.

A BBC microcomputer equipped with a Wordwise Plus word
processor chip was merely the tool with which this manuscript
was created.

ACKNOWLEDGEMENTS

I would like to say a particular thank you to the following people, Denise Randell and Mick Nadal for allowing me to include some of their materials on classroom evaluation. Tony Gray and Carl Billson of the Loughborough Micro Project (formerly the Loughborough Primary Micro Project, LPMP) for their cheerful suggestions and for the loan of some of their materials. Sarah and all the staff of the East Midlands MEP Regional Centre, and last but not least, those of my students at Loughborough who have patiently listened to and commented on my ideas.

Derek Blease
Loughborough

For Valerie, Kate

and their two furry friends

Chapter One

COMPUTERS IN SCHOOLS: AN INTRODUCTION

Since the Department of Trade and Industry introduced its Micros in Schools scheme in 1981, the number of microcomputers in our primary and secondary schools has increased at an alarming rate. The cause of this alarm is not that computers have found their way into our schools per se, but that in many cases their arrival has completely outstripped the time and resources available to those wishing to provide adequate in-service training for the teachers who are expected to use them in their classrooms. Both MEP and the Local Education Authorities have struggled, with limited resources, to provide sufficient courses to cater for the demands made by those teachers who recognise the microcomputer as an important resource, not just in the classrooms of the future, but in our classrooms now. However, there remains the more difficult problem of convincing those who have not yet recognised the potential of the computer, that there is something in this new technology for them. Microtechnology has become such an integral part of our everyday lives in both work and leisure, that it is not enough to leave it to a band of dedicated enthusiasts to introduce our children to the important social, political and ethical issues raised by its use and abuse in society. A serious problem, therefore, is that if microtechnology in general, and microcomputers in particular, are to become as integral a part of school life and the curriculum as other tools and resources, then all teachers must become confident and competent users. Perhaps realistically, the only way to achieve this objective is to ensure that computers are used in schools in such a way that the unconvinced can see the positive benefits to them, not just in a few subjects, but across the curriculum, and in their own subjects in particular. Of course this depends upon the appropriate use of the hardware and software in schools. This in turn depends on the ability of those teachers using it to make appropriate judgments about its use which are founded upon a firm base of knowledge and understanding of educational principles and issues. For inevitably, discussions and decisions about the appropriate and inappropriate use of microcomputers in schools and the curriculum, centre around the educational issues of the day, not those to do with computing itself.

COMPUTERS AND THE CURRICULUM

There is little doubt that, since the introduction of computers into schools began, more and more teachers have become enthused by what they perceive to be its possibilities. However, maintaining that initial flush of enthusiasm is not always easily achieved unless teachers learn how to discriminate between what stands up to scrutiny from an educational standpoint, and what does not. It is not that they do not already posess the knowledge and skills to do so, but it is often the case that the need to apply those skills is overshadowed in their minds by the apparent need to master the plethora of technical language printed in computer manuals and some computer journals.

It is no new thing to pronounce the hope that computers will not join the teaching machines of the 1950s and 1960s to collect dust in school cupboards. What is not so common is to hear the view expressed that educational computing should place its emphasis on the educational issues, not the computing. Of course any discussion of computers in the curriculum implies that the participants are conversant with the issues raised by their own curriculum model, whether it be their current model, or a proposed model for the needs of society in the future. Kelly (1984,pp.1-22) argues that many teachers and schools are embracing the new technology as the essence of the 2001 curriculum '...just as avidly for its 'futuristic' attractions as once they embraced the study of the ancient world for the traditional values enshrined there'. His conclusion is that the outcome of this is essentially the same, in that teachers fail to evaluate the curriculum '...in terms of its educational merits and value here and now'.

This view certainly puts one in mind of the early days of educational computing when a relatively small band of people in schools and colleges had what can only be described as a gut-feeling about the microcomputer and its impending importance in education. Fiddy (1981), describes what it was like:

> Initially the enthusiasts experimented. We wrote for ourselves, learning what the systems would do and for what they might be used in school. If the programs worked, our classes and schools used them. It was new, exciting obsessive, fascinating, creative, and wonderful in many ways, but exceedingly inefficient.

We lacked the skills to make the technology work for us. Program development could proceed only as fast as our mastery of the micros. We had to teach ourselves or seek people who could help. It was a slow process, made slower by isolation.

Meeting fellow enthusiasts now, and looking to the future, we hope for something more efficient. There is no need for newcomers to struggle so hard as we did. There is a feeling for what is wanted, how it can be produced, and the part which teachers might play in the process.

Developing high quality software is not a task for enthusiastic hobbyists. Even if you have the skills, it is too time-consuming.

At that time few had crystallised their thoughts about its place within existing curriculum models. What was more common was the hope that it might catalyse the formulation of new curriculum models geared more specifically to speculations about the needs of young people in the society of the twenty-first century. As a result of this, the pioneers of educational computing generally failed to see current use of the computer in the classroom as anything other than 'computer studies', or as something which might take over some of the teaching functions which were then, and still are today, better performed by the teachers themselves. It is only in more recent times that the quality of software and the debate about its use in the classroom have begun to catch up with the phenomenal rate at which the technology itself is developing.

There is no doubt that courses in computer awareness, information technology, and computer studies are here to stay, but what we must guard against is the tendency for these to be seen as being apart from the rest of the curriculum. In the industrial and consumer societies of the world micro-chip technology is rapidly becoming all-pervasive; wherever one looks one finds more and more examples of its application. In daily life microtechnology is something one uses, it is a tool for achieving ones objectives more quickly, more cheaply or more efficiently. It even facilitates things which, ten years ago, would have been considered impossible. Such developments must be reflected in our schools. With the exception of the small proportion of the population who will be the scientists and technologists of the future, the technology is there to be used and assimilated into our daily lives rather than to be isolated as a subject for advanced study.

Teachers, more than anyone else, need to become computer-literate, and in so doing to become confident and efficient users. Microtechnology must become as pervasive and integral a part of school life as it is rapidly becoming in the worlds of work and leisure. An important part of the way ahead is for computers to be used and to be seen to be used appropriately in schools, they should not, like so many other things in the school curriculum, be seen merely as things one is taught about.

SOFTWARE EVALUATION

There is a pressing need for teachers to develop their ability to select suitable programs. Faced with an ever-increasing mountain of so-called educational software, they must choose those programs which might, in certain circumstances, be of use to them in the classroom. Rarely is there a chance to try a program out in school before deciding whether to buy or not, although a few software publishers are helpful in this respect. The fact that the financial constraints placed upon school are ever greater makes it more and more important for teachers to be properly equipped to make such informed decisions.

In fact the term 'software evaluation' is rather misleading in this context since the very act of evaluation implies the testing of material in real classrooms with real children. What is more, such evaluations require that the programs are judged against a set of well defined criteria. These criteria must be based upon the teacher's own curriculum model which in turn determines the specific aims and objectives for a series of lessons or particular topic to be taught.

What is more appropriate is to describe the process in two stages. Firstly, Software selection; a process undertaken outside the classroom by a teacher or group of teachers who are well informed about the educational issues of computing. Decisions are made about the potential of the programs under scrutiny by critical reference to a whole series of commonly agreed criteria. These criteria might be said to constitute aspects of 'good practice' in the design and publication of educational software. Decisions must be made by individual teachers, however, according to the particular use they have in mind for the program to achieve their own specific lesson aims and objectives. What might work for one teacher in one situation might not work for another. Indeed, what might work for one teacher with one class may not work at all well for the same teacher with a different class, having different interests, needs and abilities. All experienced teachers know that this is common to all forms of lesson planning, it is not unique to the world of educational computing.

Secondly, software evaluation is a process performed in schools and classrooms, and can be extended over a considerable period of time. Careful planning is needed to integrate the use of the program into the overall plan and objectives of the scheme of work. This time the effectiveness of the program may be measured in terms of such things as learning outcomes, or its ability to maintain high levels of pupil motivation over time. However, whatever criteria are used for evaluation, they must relate directly to the aims and objectives of the teacher who is actually using the program. After all, what might appear to be a totally uninspiring program can end up as part of a most stimulating and creative lesson in the right hands.

WHY DO WE NEED TO EVALUATE SOFTWARE?

What this all leads up to, I would suggest, is that the suitability of a program can only be effectively assessed by the teacher who is intending to use it. Judgements have to be made knowing the strengths and weaknesses of the class and the rate at which individuals are able to absorb new ideas. The teacher must decide which points of the work would be best handled by the computer, and at which points it might be necessary to intervene with other tasks away from the computer. Having said this, you might wonder why any other form of software selection and evaluation might be necessary at all. The fact is, of course, that most teachers would argue that time is too short for them to do justice to every program before they use it in the classroom. This problem has been described by Spielman (1981), in a very amusing way in an article called 'Programs and Busy Teachers'. One can certainly understand this view, and so it is important that teachers come to understand how software assessments are conducted, and to be able to discriminate between those which might be reliable and those which might not. What is more, when making assessments for themselves, the criteria by which the programs are judged need to have become 'second nature' in order that teachers can make these important professional judgements in such a short space of time. If they do not have to think about what the computing issues are, they can concentrate more of their time on those issues which are essentially educational.

Acquiring the necessary skills

Without help, acquiring the experience to make such judgements can be time consuming and arduous to the extent that many would give up in the process, convinced that computers were, after all, not for them. Just a few bad experiences in the classroom with unsuitable software, which has not been fully explored before use, can seal the computer's fate to remain at the back of a dusty store cupboard.

Providing the necessary background experience to enable teachers to cope with software selection and evaluation, both their own and that of others, is best done through in-service courses. However, Jones and Preece (1984, pp.17-20), suggest that providing the necessary background experience to be able to answer many of the questions found in so called 'evaluation checklists' is just what most courses do not provide. They cite an example from one such checklist '..in order to answer the question "To what degree is the micro the best medium for achieving the program's aims and objectives?" the teacher needs a certain amount of experience of actually using the computer in teaching'. Most in-service courses, they argue, are just not long enough, or the course organisers do not recognise that developing criteria for selecting good software is difficult, and therefore fail to provide the necessary background which the teachers so desperately need. What they are leading up to, of course, is a description of their own course, one of an excellent series of 40-50 hour in-service teacher training packs produced by the Open University's Micros in Schools Project and funded by the Microelectronics Education Programme (MEP) (Open University press,1984). What follows is a brief summary of the course content to provide something of the flavour of what might be considered by many to be good practice in the area of software selection.

The aims of the course are to give teachers sufficient expertise to evaluate the design of existing software, a process, which they maintain, should include an appreciation of some general programming concepts. This first stage avoids the common mistake of perpetuating the view that all teachers should be able to program in BASIC. By concentrating on structured programming in LOGO (a programming language specifically designed for children), the course provides teachers with an insight into good programming habits while also introducing them to a very powerful classroom tool for the development of children's conceptual thinking. This activity is accompanied by the opportunity to read about and examine a wide variety of educational programs. These include programs for drill and practice, simulations, adaptive intelligent systems, information retrieval and modelling. Following this some selection criteria activities are undertaken during which teachers must decide '..what makes good software good?' Three different programs are studied in detail alongside case-studies written by teachers who have used the programs in their own classrooms, and of course the program documentation. Finally the teachers complete a software selection criteria sheet which enables them to summarise the good and bad features of each program. The whole course is accompanied with a carefully selected collection of key readings and discussion texts.

TEACHERS AND RESEARCHERS

It is generally agreed that, in the initial flush of enthusiasm for educational computing, a great deal of poor software was produced. Although there are now many good programs on the market, too few are adequately tried in classrooms before they are published. I would suggest that in some ways, educational software is suffering the same fate as that identified by Annan (1977), with regard to educational broadcasting. That is that there is a '...profound suspicion of research in educational broadcasting. Even among those who are willing to support the idea in principle, there is a distinct sense of unease about applying research in such a way that it may affect the way programs are produced'.

Clearly, the quality of discussion, if any, in much software documentation would seem to indicate that this is indeed true of many software authors and publishers. Little really objective appraisal is reported, let alone effective trials in schools. Many seem to feel that subjective impressions or mechanical checklists are adequate. Of course there are exceptions. The Loughborough Primary Micro project (LPMP) program 'The Kingdom of Helior' (Ladybird-Longman, 1985) includes a description of follow-up work done by children in a variety of schools prior to publication. Teachers' notes in this and other LPMP packages contain many ideas and suggestions taken from teachers and children in the trial schools. Similarly the 4Mation package 'Dragon World',(4MATION, 1985), is well documented with suggestions and ideas taken from teachers and children in the schools. Mike Matson, one of the production team, comments in the User's manual that 'Many people responded to requests for comments, criticisms and ideas for classroom activities'. Many of whom '...gave the software a good thrashing. Some of them still managed a polite response even when they received yet another version that didn't work'.

Perhaps some software publishers and authors see researchers as 'outsiders', with little understanding of educational issues, something which Bates (1981) calls 'professional defensiveness' when describing a similar phenomenon observed in professional broadcasters. However, the best software evaluations are done using teachers in their own classrooms or by teachers themselves. However, in the field of education there is an additional dimension. Everyone has an opinion to express about what is right or wrong with education. Just raise the question of education one evening in the local pub and you'll see what I mean. There seems to be a general feeling that ...'I've been through the system, therefore I'm an expert.' The effect may be that the professional credibility of teachers and educational researchers is somewhat diminished in many peoples' eyes. This may be true even to the extent that much so-called educational software is designed and written by people with little or no experience, or even training in education. Perhaps, for them, this 'I know what's best' attitude prevents them from seeing that there is much to be learned from the teachers' professional judgement of their work.

TEACHERS AND COMPUTERS

The introduction of computers into classrooms has brought other problems for teachers which are equally as important. Perhaps the initial reaction of many has been the fear that their jobs are about to be taken over by a machine. Very often this fear emanates from the mistaken belief that computers are, in some way, intelligent and able to do anything at the touch of a button, a view encouraged and perpetuated by popular science fiction. However, after just a little experience of the school computer, it is quite a disappointment to learn just how carefully program instructions must be spelled out to get it to perform the simplest of tasks.

Even though there is now at least one microcomputer in every school in Britain, it is a far cry from the day when they will take over the teachers' jobs. Perhaps a more pressing problem to be faced is to decide how a limited number of computers is to be fairly and efficiently shared between all those who wish to use them. In some schools the computers are mobile and are wheeled from room to room. In other schools the computers are static, and the children have to change rooms in order to use them. It is not true to say that such decisions about resources are simply to do with issues of management. There is an important difference between having one or more computers on hand for use as tools in the classroom, and having to march everyone to the 'computer room' for a lesson which will essentially be about computers. Such decisions, therefore, have a very special importance for curriculum issues regarding the relationship between teachers, computers, learners and what is learnt, which cannot be ignored.

Even when the problems of who is going to use the computers are decided in a school, there remains the problem of obtaining enough software. Schools are under pressure to cut costs, while computer software is not cheap. Consequently schools have earned the unenviable reputation of being 'hotbeds of software piracy'. The problem has become so serious that many major software publishers have threatened to pull out of the educational software business altogether. If this happens then schools will be left very much in the lurch as far as software is concerned. Even those teachers who have some knowledge of programming would not be able to supply the needs of everyone, and even if they could, it would not be desirable.

It is important that teachers should learn to apply as critical an eye to computer software as they do to other more conventional resources. No teacher would buy a set of new text books without careful scrutiny of their content, artwork and layout. This being so it is surprising to see how much software is purchased by mail order, or following a quick flick through the teachers notes. Or is it? At least with a book one can browse through its pages, dipping in here and there to sample it's contents. Computer programs are different. Apart from any teachers notes or pupil handbook, one disc or cassette looks much like any other. To scrutinise the contents properly requires considerably more commitment to the idea of purchasing the program, not to mention the extra time and effort it takes to look at how it sets out to achieve its objectives.

A VERSATILE RESOURCE

So what makes computers such an attractive proposition in such a wide variety of schools and colleges? The real computing enthusiasts will tell us that the very act of programming, whatever the language, is such a challenging and intellectually stimulating exercise, that everyone should learn to do it. While my own modest attempts at programming convince me of the truth of the former statement, I am far from being convinced of the truth of the latter. There is, of course, one exception. Many teachers encourage the use of LOGO in their classrooms, but LOGO is a programming language specifically for children. Not only that, while using LOGO children do develop an understanding of how well-structured programs work, but this is of secondary importance to the more fundamental skills and concepts which it is designed to develop. My advice to any teacher who wants to gain an insight into how programs work, is to learn how to use LOGO, and then use it in the classroom where they will gain an even greater insight into the way that children think.

So, if learning to program is a low-priority activity in all but the computer studies class, what is the key to the popularity of the computer? In a word, it is 'versatility'. With a computer the activity is determined by the software. This means that if you have a variety of programs, all doing very different things, you have a single resource which is more versatile than any other. At one moment you may have a patient tutor, at another an animated blackboard. Sometimes you will have a sophisticated data-base or a simulation of a complex scientific process, while at other times you will hold the key to intriguing adventures in imaginary worlds of dragons and witches or you may pit your wits against aliens from outer space. On other occasions you may want to control a robot or a machine or even to monitor a scientific experiment.

Let us not get too carried away with these possibilities. There are some things which computers do very well, but in the context of the classroom there are some things that they don't do as well as other more conventional resources. It is therefore an important aspect of both the selection and evaluation of software to be able to recognise these strengths and weaknesses.

WHAT ARE COMPUTERS GOOD AT?

Many people have tried to define what it is that computers do best, but we must be aware that it rather depends what your expectations are. What might seem to be stengths to mathematicians, may not be seen as such to English or history teachers. Burkhardt, Fraser and Wells (1982), a group of mathematicians, list a number of computer talents which may best match the expectations of a mathematics teacher. These are:

1. Speed of operation
2. Flexibility of response
3. Facility to use graphics
4. Timing control
5. Ability to use animation
6. Randomisation
7. External device control
8. Use of input-output devices

However, with some slight modification it is possible to produce a list which would suit a wider audience of teachers. Basically then, the computer can:

a. Perform tirelessly and patiently for long periods of time in a non-threatening manner. Children's mistakes can be removed at the press of a key. Text can be manipulated and edited to produce perfect copy. Responses can remain constant and neutral no matter for how long the exercise is attempted.

b. Perform rapid and accurate calculations. Non essential and repetitive calculations can be dealt with quickly, leaving more time for the teacher to concentrate on developing the childrens' skills of analysis and encouraging the discussion of results and ideas.

c. Store and manipulate text. Wordprocessors, data-bases and text editors enable children to rapidly explore ideas and relationships, and to formulate and test hypotheses.

d. Present information in a variety of graphical forms, including animation. Histograms, pie charts and graphs can be drawn and modified quickly and efficiently. Where movement or animation would enhance the effect it can be quickly achieved.

e. Produce seemingly endless random exercises and examples of both a textual and numerical nature. This possibility for randomisation avoids the problems of children quickly learning the answers to the exercises in a book.

f. Communicate with the outside world via many external devices and robots.

But what the computer cannot do very well is:

a. Replace teachers as caring human beings whose professional knowledge and experience enables them to match childrens' learning experiences to their needs, abilities and interests.

b. Produce maps, diagrams and pictures of sufficiently high quality to replace printed material on worksheets or in books, even if this were desirable. Those who fear that computer keyboards will replace more conventional pencil and paper tasks need not worry. Some of the best and most stimulating programs are designed to encourage children to read, research, write, test and create things for themselves away from the computer. The computer is there to enhance and stimulate, not to replace, these skills.

c. Make decisions for itself without being given precise instructions on what to do. No microcomputer is any cleverer that the program it is running at the time.

COMPUTERS, SCHOOLS AND TEACHERS

So far I have tried to establish the context of the whole exercise of evaluating computer software in educational terms. Inevitably, this has included some discussion of the scale of the problem facing teachers today. Most teachers have access to a microcomputer at some time, but have a limited budget for the purchase of software. I have suggested that teachers need to be as exacting in their requirements of computer programs as they are when choosing new school text books. I have emphasised that using the computer as a teaching aid will not replace the traditional role of the teacher as some may fear. The computer is to be seen as a teaching and learning resource, albeit a versatile one, just like any other.

The purpose of this book is to make it easier for both practising teachers and students of education to differentiate between potentially good software and the rest. However, it is hoped that teachers who have some programming expertise, and who are keen to have a go at writing programs for classroom use, will find the advice contained in this book helpful when thinking about program design.

The text is aimed at computer users, not computer experts. I would stress that a knowledge of computer programming is not a prerequisite of the effective use of the computer in the classroom, and where it is necessary to introduce computer 'jargon', it is explained fully and in straightforward language.

Chapter two addresses the problem of how we distinguish between software which is 'educational', and that which is not. However, we must realise that the 'educational value' of any exercise depends very much on the use to which it is put. This is just as true for computer programs as it is for any other resource. There are times when arcade games can perform valid educational tasks, just as popular comics can be used to advantage with some reluctant readers.

Chapter three looks at the many different kinds of programs available, and develops the idea that programs can only be evaluated in the context of their design and proposed use. Educational software comes in a variety of different forms, designed to do different jobs, and implying different relationships between the computer, the child and the teacher. A program which works well in one setting may not in another. Using descriptions and illustrations of the main variations, the educational contexts in which each type might be most suitable are discussed. This is an important step in coming to understand the nature of the evaluation process. At the same time it emphasises the need for teachers to step back to examine their own objectives before undertaking the evaluation of programs.

Chapter four consists of a detailed examination of software selection and what to look out for when choosing programs for classroom use. It is aimed at those who have to make a choice without being able to try the software with children in the classroom. The detailed examination of documentation, content, presentation, versatility and robustness are considered together with appropriate perspectives on how children learn. Once again it is emphasised that a knowledge of computer languages or programming are not necessary nor even desirable. It is not the coding which is to be evaluated, it is what appears on the screen, and it's underlying educational philosophy that is important.

Finally, chapter five is aimed at those who wish to evaluate educational software in the context of the classroom. It develops ideas about measuring childrens' progress against the objectives of both program designer and program user. It is suggested that not all program types demand the same methods. Tutorial and drill and practice programs can be evaluated in terms of skills mastered and concepts acquired, simulations involve the development of a broader view of factors or conditions which form an integral part of the system as a whole. Data-bases require the acquisition of a wide range of information handling skills in conjunction with an appreciation of what constitutes legitimate data, and what does not, and the more content-free tools such as LOGO and word processors provide the user with even wider scope for self-expression and fulfilment.

Chapter Two

WHEN DOES SOFTWARE BECOME 'EDUCATIONAL'?

In attempting to answer this question we must be aware that it
involves a problem which philosophers have debated for
generations, the nature of education itself. What is
fundamental to providing any answer, therefore, is first of all
to establish a clear idea about what we mean by education, and
whether this includes any place for the concept of training in
our discussion.

EDUCATION AND TRAINING

If we were to adopt a very simple view of education whose only
necessary condition was that some kind of learning should have
taken place, we could argue that all experience is educational.
We learn something from all our experiences, and this of course
includes all experiences with computer software. However, this
clearly does not fit the generally accepted, though rarely
clarified, view of education held by many in our society. If it
did there would hardly seem to be a need for such elaborate
measures to prepare candidates for the teaching profession.
What is more, it has become quite unfassionable to talk of
'teacher training' as a process of preparing new teachers, the
term 'teacher education' being much more acceptable, especially
among those involved. So, there must be something about
education which sets it apart from merely learning something,
and makes it different from being trained. A possible
refinement of our definition could be to say that educational
experiences must bring about the development of desirable
qualities in people. However, who is to say which qualities are
desirable, and which are not. Anthropologists are quick to
remind us that such value judgements are very culture-specific.
In other words, qualities deemed desirable in one culture may
well be considered highly undesirable in another. We don't need
to look at other societies, not even the so called primitive
ones, to see this. Examples are all around us, cultural
differences in values and attitudes being common in any complex

14

society. Indeed, definitions of what is educational and what is not can vary quite considerably in any one society, particularly between teachers, politicians and parents, but also between different groups of teachers. While these differences contribute to a healthy on-going debate about the very nature of education and provide the springboard for interesting and novel innovations, they can also lead to a great deal of confusion. Hirst and Peters (1970, pp.17-25) describe the concept of 'education' as 'a very fluid one'. Starting from the older and undifferentiated concept referring to 'any process of bringing up or rearing in which the connection either with what is desirable or with knowledge is purely contingent'., they move on to a more recent and more specific concept, suggesting that such processes are linked with 'the development of states of a person that involve knowledge and understanding in depth and breadth', as well as being desirable. Perhaps for our purposes this kind of definition of education is quite adequate since the call of education in breadth and depth is one commonly heard in educational circles these days, particularly with reference to discussions about the introduction of information technology and associated courses in schools today. So, where does this leave training. Training is more commonly asociated with the more mechanical process of acquiring certain skills not necessarily associated with understanding. Although this is something of a simplification it cannot be said that some of the activities which go on in our schools are not a kind of training. Furthermore, our experience with teaching machines and programmed learning shows that, in one of its modes at least, the computer can be as efficient a means of certain kinds of training as any other.

DIFFERENT VIEWS OF EDUCATION

As I have already said, there are many differences of opinion in our society about what education really is. The continuing debates about education and the criticism of schools and the teaching profession concerning declining standards and the lack of discipline points to some important differences between the views of the teachers and certain other sections of society. It is probably true to say that at least some of these differences arise from poor communication between schools and parents. Perhaps it is not so surprising that large sections of the population are not familiar with current educational ideas and practices. Parents and teachers alike are bombarded with advertising claims for the educational value of so many things, among which are home computers and their associated software. Teachers are better equipped to judge such claims on the basis of their specialist knowledge and experience, but what chance does this leave many parents? In the software market potential

'Educational' software

buyers of home computers are lured by claims that they are 'educational'. If one takes a closer look at the kinds of software on offer it is easy to see how so many outdated views of education are perpetuated.

SOFTWARE FOR SALE

I recently spent half an hour in each of two major national high street stores where home computers and software are sold. Both stores had several display shelves of software which could be roughly divided into small business packages, arcade games, and programs which claimed some direct 'educational' function or value. In the 'education' category this is what I found:

Pan Course tutors in French, Chemistry, Physics and Biology. These are advertised as 'integrated study and revision courses for GCE 'O' level'.

Longman 'O' level and CSE revision courses in Computer studies and Mathematics.

Collins Gem revision software in Biology, Physics and Chemistry for GCE 'O' level and CSE.

Collins Software 'First numbers', and 'Know your tables'.

Mirror Soft 'Look sharp' for developing observation skills and visual memory.

Ivan Berg software 'History: 20th century'.

Acornsoft 'Tree of knowledge'. An educational database to teach categorisation skills.

Five Ways software 'Learning box' for basic reading and number skills.

Good Housekeeping software 'Mr.T's measuring games'.

Macmillan 'Learn to read series' parallel to the 'Gay way readers'.

Penguin study software 'Shakespeare: Twelfth Night and Romeo and Juliet' for 'O' level and CSE.

Celtic revision software for examination practice and tests in Biology, Chemistry and Physics for GCE 'O' level.

Tawny Software, Compututor 'Basic arithmetic'.

Sci CAL software Physics series,
'Images' a simulation program for ray diagrams.

Pitmansoft 'keyboard skills'.

Various versions of LOGO.

With only three exceptions, 'Tree of knowledge', 'Images'
and LOGO, all of the so called educational programs on display
were of the tutorial or drill and practice type. While there is
nothing wrong with tutorial and drill and practice programs as
such, indeed they are used in classrooms at times when teachers
decide they are appropriate, they do not represent or reflect
the much wider variety of software used in our classrooms
today. In fact, it is reasonable to say that such programs do
least to exploit the full potential of the computer as an
educational resource. I will be taking up the question of
different kinds of software in chapter three, but it is
worthwhile to note that Britain leads the world in the
production of quality educational software, and it is only in
British schools that one can see such a variety of versatile
and high quality software being used. Tutorial and drill and
practice programs, which still dominate the American market,
form only a small part of the range available to British
teachers and children.

If such a limited range of types of software are available
for home use, it is not surprising that some parents believe
that all education is, or at least should be, like that.
Furthermore, mediocre examples of such programs are really
quite easy to write, and seeing what is available on the
shelves, aspiring programmers attempt to emulate them. The
result is that even more tutorial and drill and practice
programs become available.

A MECHANISTIC VIEW OF EDUCATION

What view of education do these high street packages imply? I
have already suggested that they are not representative of the
programs in use in our classrooms, and so it might be
reasonable to assume that they imply a rather outdated
educational philosophy. Behaviourist theories of learning
predominate to the exclusion of the cognitive and affective
aspects which are more common in educational thinking today.
Perhaps they reflect a common and very simplistic view of what
education is. We return to the 'I've been through the system
therefore I know what's best' syndrome discussed in chapter
one. It often manifests itself by depicting education merely as
a process of rote learning and drill and practice, accompanied
by the view that teachers should get on and make the children

do it.

Of course serious students and practitioners appreciate that this is not the essence of education at all. The acquisition of most fundamental skills and concepts requires a lot more than just rote learning, and the whole process of education, as they see it, is much more complex.

One problem is that the high street package is generally easy to use, requiring little time to learn how to get it going. While this may be a strength in one sense, it is also a serious weakness. No program that is going to be highly versatile across the curriculum is going to be mastered in five minutes. For example, a reasonably sophisticated database like INFORM (Nottinghamshire C.C.1983) or QUEST (AUCBE, 1983) requires much longer for an experienced teacher to explore and consider all the classroom applications even if it were possible. It is impossible to learn and fully exploit the possibilities of LOGO in a few hours. No program that is really able to extend childrens' abilities to think and formulate solutions to problems can be mastered in five minutes. This is not to say that good examples of such programs are obscure and difficult to understand as such, it is just that the available options and possibilities are so wide that they cannot all be considered in such a short space of time.

Having said all this, we must not underestimate the value of tutorial and drill and practice programs in their place. They are widely used in schools, but they do need a teacher's knowledge and experience in choosing the right program at the right time. For example, spelling and visual matching exercises must be fully integrated into the child's scheme of work. The idea that you can sit a child at the computer with any old program, and let the computer do the work is very unsatisfactory from an educational point of view.

In fact of the two, drill and practice programs are the more common since tutorial programs are a little too much like the programmed learning of the 1950s and 1960s. One of their major weaknesses is that their content and sequence is rather formal and fixed, making individual programs rather narrow in application. However with the increasing availability of authoring systems like Author (ESM,1984) teachers are able to construct quickly specific tutorials to suit their own requirements. All without the need to know anything about programming.

COMPUTERS AND EDUCATIONAL OBJECTIVES

I have so far suggested that the processes of software selection and evaluation cannot go on without taking cognisance of our specific objectives for a lesson or series of lessons. Having said this I am aware that, despite its recent revival in the National Criteria for the General Certificate of Secondary

Education, (GCSE), in Britain, the 'objectives' or 'systems' approach to curriculum planning has been much criticised in recent years. However, in thinking about how we might consider objectives in helping us to select and evaluate software for classroom use we can benefit from taking on board at least some of the ideas of those advocating such an approach to curriculum design.

By 'objectives' I simply mean statements of what the pupils are intended to do or learn. This implies more than just specifying the content of a lesson, since it is essential to decide what skills and processes are to be carried out, thus determining the nature of the actual 'activities' of the lesson.

One of the earliest advocates of the 'objectives' approach was Tyler (1949), who argued that teachers and curriculum planners must specify both curriculum content and the processes and skills to be used and developed in dealing with that content. This was followed by Bloom's Taxonomy of Educational Objectives, a most influential work, published in two volumes (Bloom,1956. Krathwohl, Bloom and Masia, 1964). The classification was into three domains:

1. The cognitive domain, concerned with intellectual knowledge and skills.

2. The affective domain, concerned with feelings, attitudes and values.

3. The psychomotor domain, concerning physical skills.

Bloom and Krathwohl's taxonomies are essentially hierarchical descriptions of 'levels of competence' or 'levels of mastery'. For example, it is suggested that cognitive development follows a sequence from knowledge (of specific facts or procedures or classifications etc.) through comprehension of the knowledge, its applications in particular situations, to the higher order mental skills of analysis, synthesis and evaluation, all of which are involved in the problem-solving process.

In the affective domain there is also a sequential developmental flavour. Starting with attending to specific phenomena, then responding to them, and then learning to value them, and organising ones values relative to one another to finally create ones own personalised 'value system'.

If we apply a similarly heirarchical progression to the development of the physical skills in the psychomotor domain, we can see how applications of the microcomputer can be used to great effect with the very young and the physically or mentally handicapped in the development of the visual-motor skills so essential to the manipulation of small objects, writing and keyboard operation. Starting with the 'reflexive skills', simple repetitive stimulus-response types of activity involving little or no planning, the progression leads on to the 'planning-intensive' skills which involve complex decision-making at the conscious or subconscious level.

A good example of a thoroughly prescriptive theory of instruction is that of Bruner (1966). He sets forth rules for effective learning, rules which, in turn, provide a standard for evaluating any particular way of teaching and learning. Bruner's contribution to social studies is a good example of its application. 'Man a course of study' (MACOS) (See Bruner 1966, chapters 4 and 8) includes films, slides, tapes, written presentations, detailed guides, and a special training course for teachers. If microcomputers and software had been available at the time, no doubt they would have been specified also. Although still in use in some British schools, the results of MACOS and similar programmes have frequently been disappointing.

Gagne (1970, 1974. Gagne and Briggs, 1974) sets out meticulously his theoretical basis and prescriptions for action right down to the planning of individual lessons. His assumption is that the human brain itself works rather like a computer, coding information from the environment and transforming it. Like Bloom, Gagne saw the classification as hierarchical, from simple stimulus-response conditioning to problem-solving. At each level the performance was specified which would indicate that learning had taken place.

Perhaps the most distinctive thing about an objective is that it is a statement of what the children ought to be able to do after the lesson. What would be more practicable when deciding upon objectives would be to concentate on processes only omitting content altogether. A good example of this, where computers are not involved, is the Schools Council 'Science 5-13' project (Ennever and Harlen, 1972), whose objectives, unlike those of MACOS, were expressed as processes in science which could be applied to any content.

More recently the GCSE 'General Criteria', and the more specific 'Subject Criteria' are similarly expressed as processes. To continue with the example of science for a moment, pupils are expected to have, amongst other things, a knowledge and understanding of 'scientific and technological applications with their social, economic and environmental implications'. Similarly, they are expected to exhibit the skills and abilities to 'explain technological applications of science and evaluate associated social, economic and environmental implications'. These are just two out of many objectives which have great relevance to microeletronics and information technology.

In discussing content, the national criteria make the position quite clear:

> There is more science that is intelligible, relevant and interesting to secondary school students than could be accommodated realistically within a course covering as many as three GCSE science syllabuses. For science to make a valuable contribution to a balanced education, a judicious selection has to be made from this vast body of knowledge. The number of justifiable ways of making such a selection is large and it is the more important, therefore, to ensure that the content of any syllabus provides an appropriate vehicle for the realisation of the Aims and Assessment objectives'. (GCSE National Criteria for Science. January 1985, p.4)

By formulating our objectives in this way, in terms of processes, without specific reference to content, we are constantly reminded of our basic aims which, in turn, provide a framework within which the best methods and content can be chosen to suit the situation. However, other alternatives have been suggested.

Eisner (1969) suggests that the objectives approach is unsatisfactory because it implicitly claims to predict student 'responses' to 'stimuli' provided by the lesson. This is more acceptable, he argues, when all that is required is the reproduction of what is presented, but when the learner's active participation is sought, something different is required. Predicted objectives are insufficient when judging creative work in say writing or art, their value is best judged retrospectively on the basis of principles appropriate to what the learner has attempted to do. Eisner suggests that what he calls 'expressive objectives', describing educational encounters would be more appropriate. An expressive objective 'identifies a situation in which children are to work, a problem with which they are to cope, a task in which they are to engage; but it does not specify what from that encounter, situation, problem or task they are to learn'. Such 'expressive objectives' are not objectives at all in the sense we have used the word up to now. Instead of specifying a new competence or knowledge that will be learnt, they specify the activity which the learners will be engaged in, which in turn specifies the situation which the teacher must set up. It is at this point that decisions can be made about the possible role that a computer program might play. In this respect, argues Barnes (1982,p.59), 'it is closer to teachers' traditional ways of planning' than a straightforward objectives approach. 'Most of all, it recognises the learner's contribution to his own learning, and does not treat him as a passive receiver'.

This is not unlike Stenhouse's (1975) 'procedural principles', where the focus is upon the modes of learning appropriate to different kinds of knowledge. He argues that the area of knowledge to be taught carries with it implicit principles of procedure which govern learning, and therefore teaching, in that subject. We will return to these ideas in later chapters when we discuss the suitability of different kinds of programs for the development of different kinds of skills and concepts, and when we look at Stenhouse's ideas about 'teachers as researchers' when evaluating software in the classroom.

COMPUTERS AND PSYCHOLOGY

Historically, educational computing has followed in the footsteps of programmed learning. In other words, the first attempts to use computers in the classroom were most often as some form of 'teaching machine' using tutorial programs of either a linear or a branching kind. Really, the only difference between this and the mechanical teaching machines of the 1950s and 1960s was that the individual 'frames' appeared on a television screen, and, because the computer was able to react relatively quickly, branching programs gave the appearance of being 'interactive'. I think, however, that it is probably more accurate to say that such crude programs were more 'reactive' than 'interactive' in that the responses were fixed and were unable to adapt to unusual or unexpected inputs from the user. A branching program can create the illusion of being versatile and 'interactive' simply by virtue of the number of branches available, but if the user follows the same path again, the same old responses will appear. In more recent times tutorial and drill and practice programs have come to be used in classrooms as aids to teachers and children at times when they are appropriate. As I have already said, these programs do perform an important function, but equally, they do not fully exploit the potential of the microcomputer as a teaching and learning aid. In a sense their limitations correspond to the limitations of the psychological theory of learning upon which they are based, namely those of behaviourism.

THE BEHAVIOURIST THEORIES OF LEARNING

Of all contemporary behaviourists, the American psychologist, B.F.Skinner, is probably the best known. This is especially true in education because of his contribution to programmed learning. Skinner was primarily interested in conditioning, and more particularly, his own version which he called 'operant conditioning'. His experiments with both rats and pigeons led him to the conclusion that learning begins with a certain amount of exploration or trial and error until, by chance, some positive event occurs. This was usually achieved by giving the animal food when it pressed a lever. After a few such chance contacts bringing reward, the behaviour pattern would change dramatically, obtaining a reward every time. This was the sign that learning had taken place. What was important about Skinner's work was that it demonstrated instrumental or 'operant' behaviour whereby the learner produces its own reward or reinforcement by converting what was a productive accident into a behaviour pattern which was intentional. Following many experiments with both animals and humans Skinner was able to list four important things he had discovered about learning:

(a) Each step in the learning process should be short and should grow out of previously learned behaviour.
(b) In the early stages, learning should be regularly rewarded and at all stages carefully controlled by a schedule of continuous and/or intermittent reinforcement.
(c) Reward should follow quickly when the correct response appears. This is referred to as feedback and is based on the principle that motivation is enhanced when we are informed of our progress. This is allied to (a) since to ensure a high success rate the steps in the learning process must be sufficiently small and within the capacities of the learner.
(d) The learner should be given an opportunity to discover stimulus discriminations for the most likely path to success. (Child, 1981, p.89)

When this is applied to the planning of a linear teaching program a number of essential requirements arise which could well apply to tutorial and drill and practice computer programs as well. Those requirements are:

(a) Small pieces of subject matter presented in a logical sequence at such a pace as to pretty well guarantee success on the part of the pupil.
(b) Active responses on the part of the learner. This, called 'constructed response', usually entails writing a word or phrase in answer to a question. (or in the case of a computer program, typing in a word or phrase, or responding to a multiple-choice question by choosing a number and pressing return. My comment in brackets.)
(c) Immediate knowledge of the accuracy of the response, which is usually correct if (a) is followed.
(d) The pupils can work at their own pace.
(Child, 1981, p.104)

Branching programs depend very much upon the same ideas, but are more sophisticated in that they provide for opportunities to follow different routes. They also allow for what are called 'remedial loops' which enable certain sections to be studied for longer if the learner is having difficulties.

Psychologists, like Skinner, who support behaviourist theories of learning are not particularly concerned about knowing what happens inside an organism when learning takes place. Since these intervening variables are not available for direct observation, they do not figure in explanations of how learning occurs. It is the observable and modifiable stimuli and responses which control and delineate behaviour that are considered important. While this is fine for relatively simple examples of learning, it leaves many questions unanswered about the organism's perception of a situation as a basis for responding to stimulation. It is for this reason that behaviourist theories of learning are only applicable to the design of software which performs the simplest tasks like tutorials and drill and practice. If we are to understand the thinking that lies behind programs which require children to be creative, or develop strategies for action, or to formulate and test hypotheses, we must turn to other, more complex theories which concentrate on the cognitive aspects of learning.

COGNITIVE THEORIES OF LEARNING

The behaviourists and their theories have been criticised because the nature of the learning situations that they set up for their subjects, whether they be animals or humans, are so difficult that they can do little else but learn by trial and error. The criticism was raised in the light of what psychologists know about 'intuitive' learning, or learning through 'insight', and suggests that the approach an individual adopts to learning at any one time all depends upon the context in which the problem is being solved. So, the stimulus which spurs the problem-solver on is not just the problem, but also its context. This point is important to us in our study of computer software because, as teachers, we often need to create an appropriate context in which a problem is to be solved just so that children can be encouraged into tackling the problem in a particular kind of way. On one occasion this might involve practical work in a laboratory, or it might require evidence to be sought from original documents, or on some occasions it may be more appropriate to construct a computer data-file. Theories which involve 'insight' as a mechanism of learning, sometimes called gestalt theories, emphasise the importance of adaptability in the use of existing knowledge to form new insights rather than the mechanical reception of stimulus-response bonds.

Probably the psychologist who has had the greatest influence on the world of education is Piaget, whose theories of cognitive development have had a profound effect upon the way teachers structure childrens' classroom experience. Following closely in his footsteps in educational computing is

Papert, who, having worked alongside Piaget, has applied Piaget's theories to the study of how children can be encouraged to use computers to explore relationships and to solve problems.

For Piaget, the development of thinking skills starts with simple sensory and motor activities, gradually being superseded by internal representations of actions carried out by the child. This is followed, through the use of language, by higher forms of logical thinking, firstly using objective evidence, and finally mental reasoning. Conceptual growth occurs because the child, while actively attempting to adapt to the environment, organises actions into what he calls 'schemata', through processes which he has termed 'assimilation' and 'accommodation'. It is an 'active' rather than a 'passive' view of the part played by children in their own development, whereby self-directed motor activity is an important aspect of cognitive development. 'Schemata' are actions which become organised into distinct patterns of behaviour, the formation of which depend upon action on the part of the child in attempting to adapt to the demands of the environment. 'Assimilation' occurs as the child incorporates new perceptions either to form new schemata or to integrate them into existing ones. However, as the child becomes able to modify existing schemata to allow for new environmental demands 'accommodation' is said to have taken place. For Piaget, this all occurs as a part of a maturational and hierarchical process whereby concept formation follows an invariant pattern through a series of clearly definable stages which must be experienced and passed through in a set order.

'Representational schemata' are formed when symbols (numbers, words etc.) finally replace actions, and so when the child achieves a mental representation of the world by means of memory, imagery and symbolic language, 'internalisation' of these experiences has been achieved. This all sounds quite involved, and after all this is not a text book on psychology. However, as we explore the implications of Piaget's work for teaching, you will see that it has great importance for our understanding of the processes of software selection and evaluation, particularly when we come to ask the question as to whether the children are equipped to operate at the intellectual level demanded by the program.

PIAGET AND COMPUTER PROGRAMS

Although some of Piaget's ideas have been criticised, his work has had an indisputable influence on educational thinking. Rather than go into the weak spots in this rather 'potted account' of his work, we will concentrate more on those useful aspects which have a direct bearing on our interest as users of computer software in classrooms.

The maturational and hierarchical development of conceptual skills has important implications for all curriculum design, not just for the use of computer software. What Piaget's theory implies is that certain periods are critical in mental growth. A classic example of where this was not fully taken into account (Shayer and Adey 1981), is the planning of Nuffield Science courses. It has been demonstrated that, on many occasions, pupils are confronted with problems and concepts which require levels of thinking which only the most able in their age group can achieve. Although, in theory, this might be argued to provide a stimulus for the further conceptual development of the rest, in practice, the scheme has only been demonstrated to be really effective with the most able pupils. Similarly, when choosing software for children we must be aware of their marurational level, and, especially if it is our intention to use the computer as a means to developing their conceptual skills further, we must be careful in our choice so as not to make too great a demand on them too quickly.

Programs for use in junior and lower secondary schools should involve concrete experiences and activities, building up, where appropriate, to more abstract reasoning. Programs which encourage children to conduct live experiments, use other resources like books and workpacks, collect data from the real world, or to conduct paper and pencil tasks are ideal for this. Practical work is very much in keeping with Piaget's view that concept formation is the result of the internalisation of actions. To build up schemata, children require practical experience of concrete situations, which will in turn encourage assimilation and accommodation. In the early stages of learning to form and test hypotheses, explanation should accompany experience (Bruner, 1966), since children may need help in realising how hypotheses are reached. Certainly if the computer is to be used as one resource among many, these kinds of programs will fit neatly into the kind of lesson planning currently practiced by many teachers.

For those with special education needs in our secondary schools abstract thinking may never be satisfactorily attained. When choosing software for use in the remedial class this must be taken very much into account. Any abstract concepts that are involved must be carefully considered by the teacher in the light of what is known about what individual pupils can do, before introducing the program into the classroom.

If, as Piaget suggests, cognitive development is a process which depends on what has gone before, teachers must carefully select computer programs alongside other resources and activities to regulate the difficulty level and order of presentation of material. Given that most classes will contain children of mixed ability, the needs of individuals will be different for most of the time. This being so, the computer may be used on some occasions for different purposes with different children, although they may appear to be engaged in similar kinds of work.

Concept formation is considerably aided by opportunities to verbalise one's ideas. Many good computer programs can provide for this if the teacher encourages children to work together in small groups, discussing possible strategies before putting them to the test. This can be further extended by providing opportunities for creative expression through writing, art and craftwork and through drama. A good example of this is the Ladybird-Longman program 'Sheepdog', a seemingly simple program where a dog is given instructions on where to move in order to put one or two sheep into a pen. One great value of this program is that it can be used with a whole class or a small group of children who are encouraged to explore, through language, all the possible instructions which might be appropriate to achieve each particular move. This is, in essence, the beginnings of learning how to hypothesise. The chosen instruction, or hypothesis, is then put to the test by trying it to see what happens. Verbal interaction is an important communication channel by which we come to define our world. These skills can be further developed with young children using LOGO, which we will discuss briefly in the next section, and with older children, the skills of hypothetico-deductive reasoning (Popper, 1959), using such things as data-bases (Ross, 1984).

PAPERT'S LOGO

Although it is Piaget whose name is associated with the theory, it is Papert's name and his book 'Mindstorms' (Papert, 1980), which are associated with its application to educational computing. Papert has criticised much of what is done with computers in schools because it has encouraged the child to be programmed by the computer instead of the computer to be programmed by the child. This does not mean that everyone should be learning to program in Basic, as we will see, but it does raise an important point which we will look at again later, in more detail. That is that probably the most versatile, stimulating and useful programs are those which can be used as a tool by children to explore a variety of situations or problems. Papert demonstrates that it is possible to design computers to enable children to use them easily, and in so doing, he argues, the way in which they learn other things changes. At the heart of Papert's ideas is a sophisticated programming language called LOGO, which was designed specially for children. But LOGO is more than just a programming language (Martin, 1983), it is also a theory about thinking and programming. The programming process is seen as an analogy of the thinking process as Piaget described it. The development of children's thinking abilities is seen as a process whereby simple structures are generated and tested, and later combined with other simple structures to form a more abstract and complex structure. Finally, LOGO can be seen as a philosophy of education:

> The parallelism between LOGO activity and thinking lies at the base of the 'LOGO approach' to education. In developing his powers of thinking, the child builds up structures of thought by exploration of the world around him. Thus, faced with the challenge of a new problem or situation, concepts previously mastered are combined to produce a new insight, one which can then be transferred to the child's thinking about similar situations. The proponents of this view of intellectual development place emphasis on exploration and discovery as important elements in learning, and these are generally accepted as essential parts of the experience which the primary school can offer.(Martin, 1983, pp.2-6)

APPEALING EDUCATIONAL PROGRAMS

There is no doubt that, excluding business software, the most popular programs are the arcade type games. Despite a limited range of themes their appeal seems universal, crossing both political and cultural boundaries throughout the world. Unlike educational programs, they can command a big market which means big business and big profits for those who produce and market them. For this reason they are able to attract some of the most talented programmers, some of whom are very young and self taught. In the world of home computing some of these programs represent the 'state of the art' in terms of visual appeal through clever use of graphics and animation. However, there must be more to their appeal than clever graphics, and some people believe that there are lessons to be learnt from them which could help both the designers and the users of educational programs. One such person is Thomas Malone (Malone, T. 1982), who has developed a set of guidelines for designing 'highly motivating educational software', based upon a systematic study of more than a hundred people playing computer games. The study, which was conducted in the United States, was primarily concerned with what made the games fun. Using a list of 25 popular games he was able to show which game features were most and least popular with his subjects.

Arranged in rank order, and starting with the most popular, this is what he found:

1. The game has a distinct goal
2. The computer keeps a record
3. The program includes sound
4. The game involves randomness
5. The speed of answers counts
6. The program includes visual effects
7. The game involves competition
8. There are variable levels of difficulty
9. The program involves cooperation
10. The program involves fantasy

Arising from this Malone constructed his guidelines by dividing the characteristics that he believed to make instructional environments interesting, under three headings, challenge, fantasy and curiosity:

Challenge
In providing challenge, does the activity set a clear goal? If it does not, can students determine appropriate goals for themselves?
Does the activity set goals which can be personally meaningful?
Is the level of difficulty of the exercise variable, and are there multiple goal levels?
Does the exercise include random elements and selectively reveal hidden information?

Fantasy
Is the fantasy emotionally appealing?
Does the fantasy relate intrinsically to the skill to be learned in the activity? In other words, is the problem presented in terms of fantasy-world elements in which the players receive natural constructive feedback?
Does the fantasy provide a useful metaphor or analogy to help the learner apply old knowledge in understanding new things?

Curiosity
Does the program use visual effects and sound as decoration, to enhance fantasy, as a reward or as a representation system?
Are there surprises included in the program?
Does the user receive constructive feedback?

Clearly this most accurately reflects the American market since a major part of Malone's check list is better suited to the design and evaluation of drill and practice programs. However, there are ways in which it can be applied to more sophisticated educational programs. Indeed, Malone himself refers to this when discussing activities which are challenging:

> Thus, simple games, to be challenging, should probably have a single fixed goal. More complex environments (like graphics editors or computer programming languages) should be designed so that users can easily generate goals of appropriate difficulty. For example, in the LOGO system students can program a moving 'turtle' to draw designs on a computer screen or on the floor. The attractiveness of this environment is the ease with which children think of things they would like a moving turtle to do. But unless beginners have some help evaluating the difficulty of possible projects, they might often choose tasks that are discouragingly difficult. (p.32)

The ability for users to determine realistic goals for themselves seems to me to be the key to the successful use of many, so called, content-free tools. Programs like data-bases, word processors, text editors and music and graphics editors all require some sort of goal to be set which is external to the program itself. 'Since a good tool is designed to achieve goals that are already present in the external task, it does not need to provide a goal. Furthermore, since the outcome of the external goal is already uncertain, the tool itself should be reliable, efficient and usually invisible'.(p.33). In addition to achieving externally determined goals when using such tools, it is very often the case that the process of formulating realistic goals gives rise to the acquisition and practice of a variety of valuable skills in their own right. This is particularly evident in the use of data-bases where children must master a whole range of decision-making and information handling skills long before a data-file can be constructed and interrogated. In many cases this is good enough reason for using such data-base programs in the classroom irrespective of the benefits to be gained from the use of the tool in its own right.

Chapter Three

DIFFERENT KINDS OF PROGRAMS: A CASE OF HORSES FOR COURSES

If 'versatility' is the key to the microcomputer's popularity, it follows that a full and detailed understanding of the variety of uses to which it might be put is an important prerequisite for effective software selection and evaluation. In other words, I am suggesting that unless teachers are experienced in the use of all kinds of educational software they will find it very difficult to decide what would be the most appropriate use in any particular situation. The processes of selecting and evaluating software carry with them the implication that the teacher is equipped to weigh up the good and bad points of a program by reference to the range of possible alternatives available, and the variety of different ways to tackle the same problem in the classroom, of which using the computer may only be one.

There have been many attempts to classify computer aided learning into types which satisfactorily take into account the variety of learning styles to be observed in our classrooms. Maddison (1982), lists six:

1. By subject. This is not very useful when discussing general principles of educational computing, but it is helpful when classifying programs.

2. By mode of presentation. This refers to the relationship between teacher, learner and computer. It raises the question of who or what is in control of the learning process, does it go along at a pace set by the computer, the learner or by the teacher?

3. By internal technique. Some techniques and ideas are common to several kinds of computer aided learning, Maddison includes such things as 'models and simulations', 'chance and probability' and 'information retrieval'.

4. By educational paradigm. The four paradigms, or theoretical models, 'instructional', 'revelatory', 'conjectural' and

'emancipatory' all relate to the major function or purpose of a program. We will return to a more detailed discussion of these in the next section.

5. By psychological theory. As we established in chapter 2, the major division here is between programs based upon the behaviourist theories on the one hand, and those based upon the cognitive theories on the other.

6. By clarity of structure. Maddison distinguishes between programs which give no indication of their internal workings, so called 'black boxes', and those which are relatively transparent, what he calls 'glass boxes'. The suggestion is that the difference will affect how the teacher chooses to handle them in the classroom. (pp.66-67)

Of all these methods, probably the most satisfactory is that which classifies computer aided learning and therefore computer programs, by educational paradigm, originally proposed by Kemmis, Atkin and Wright (1977).

The instructional paradigm

This paradigm should be quite familiar to us since we have already considered programs which depend upon a behaviourist perspective in chapter two. However, it is worthwhile just reminding ourselves of the main features of such programs. At the heart of this paradigm lies Skinner's theory of operant conditioning. Subject material is broken down into many small learning tasks so that the learner can concentrate on each one in turn. Regular rewards or reinforcement accompany the successful completion of each task. If problems are encountered at any stage, the learner spends more time on that stage, or is routed round a 'remedial loop' in the program, providing extra help and tuition until the task has been mastered. The important thing about programs of this type is to divide the subject material up into small enough parts that the learner almost invariably achieves success first time. This is all summed up in a comment by Rushby, (1979), which still holds true to the present day:

> Skinner's original theory has since been modified and embodied as part of other more complex theories, but still can be seen as the basis of much present-day programmed learning which seeks to rationalise the teaching/learning process, sequencing the presentation of material and emphasising feedback to the student on his performance. The focus of the instruction is on the subject material and on the student's mastery of the various facts and concepts within it. (pp.22-23)

This paradigm, then, covers what we have called 'tutorial' programs, but it also includes 'drill and practice' as well. In this case the learner receives a structured succession of exercise questions which are intended to give him practice in a particular technique. These exercises can be generated in two ways. Probably the least flexible are those which form part of an 'item bank', a collection of fixed questions or exercises which are built into the program itself. Unless the list is very long, the possible exercises soon become exhausted. This can be improved by having different sets of fixed exercises stored in different data-files which can be loaded when required. The second method is for the computer to generate 'random' examples or exercises, something which computers can do very well. This way, within the broad limits of options set by the program itself, a very wide range of exercises can be presented to the learner with little fear of them being regularly repeated. It is also possible, but unfortunately uncommon, for such programs to be 'diagnostic', in the sense that incorrect responses can be monitored by the computer, which can then offer remedial help if the learner experiences consistent difficulties at any one level.

The revelatory paradigm

The essence of 'revelatory' programs is that the student is encouraged to explore a model whose subject matter and underlying theory remains hidden within the computer itself. The model is progressively 'revealed' as the student goes through a process of discovery learning. The most common forms of this type are simulations of imaginary worlds as a stimulus for language development, problem solving skills or hypothesis formation, or simulations of scientific experiments and processes. Although there is no substitute for first-hand practical experience, especially in science, such simulations are used in situations where first-hand experience would be either too expensive, too dangerous, too time-consuming or because the process is so complex that, at least initially, understanding is more effectively achieved using a simplified representation. Such simulations depend upon underlying models which have been determined by the program designer, and are not readily available for modification by the user. This illustrates an important difference between using simulations where the program allows the user to experiment by changing a number of variables to see what would happen within the confines of a fixed model, and model building itself, which is a more complex process involving the need to write one's own computer programs, and which lies outside the scope of the revelatory paradigm altogether.

The conjectural paradigm

Programs of the 'conjectural' kind provide an excellent example of the application of a cognitive view of learning to educational computing. Based upon the idea that students can be the agents of their own learning, they are provided with the facility to manipulate and test ideas and hypotheses, whilst supported by the computer which is very much under the student's control. Rushby (1979) sums up the essence of the conjectural paradigm in such a way that it almost anticipates many of the stimulating ideas of Papert's 'Mindstorms' (1980), published a year later:

> Because in the conjectural form of CAL (computer assisted learning), it is the student who is in control of the learning rather than the other way about, he is brought much closer to instructing or programming the computer than in the instructional or revelatory forms. This does not necessarily imply that the student and his teachers will tell the computer what to do - program it - with a general purpose programming language. It may be convenient and appropriate to do so, but often it is more satisfactory to provide a simpler means of controlling the computer, and one which has been designed specifically for this educational purpose. (p.31)

Just the time to introduce LOGO one might think.

Of course, science and mathematics are not the only areas of the curriculum where it is important to be able to formulate and test hypotheses. There are many opportunities for this in the humanities too, at both the primary and secondary levels. Geography, history and social studies can generate enormous quantities of data which lends itself to interrogation using a data-base program. Hypotheses can be formulated about possible relationships between items of data, which time alone would have made impossible to investigate by more conventional methods. In a sense, this 'time-saving' function of some computer programs conveniently leads us on to the 'emancipatory paradigm'.

The emancipatory paradigm
This final type is perhaps less concerned with 'teaching' and 'learning' as such, than with reducing the workload so that teaching and learning can take place free of the incidental, though often time consuming, processing of data. McDonald, Atkin, Jenkins and Kemmis (1977), have distinguished between two types of labour in this context. Firstly there is what they call 'authentic labour', which is integral to the learning task, and secondly, there is 'inauthentic labour', which is not an integral part of the learning process but may be an essential accessory to it. The best examples of this are those programs which provide facilities for calculation or information retrieval. A scientific or economic simulation might require a large amount of inauthentic labour in the form of long and laborious calculations to be performed before the student can concentrate on the interpretation of the results. The social scientist or historian may require large numbers of

census returns to be sorted and compared before important social trends become evident. The computer is an ideal tool for performing such tasks. Indeed, using a computer in this way has facilitated the inclusion of certain problems which previously could not have been studied because time was too short to complete the large amounts of data processing involved, by more conventional means.

A CASE STUDY: COMPUTERS IN UPPER SCHOOLS

Using these four educational paradigms as a guide, Roberts and Ewan (1984), attempted to assess the extent to which six schools were meeting the demands of two basic presuppositions;

1. There will be pervasive changes in society emanating from the implementation and advancement of technology based on micro-electronics.

2. Society will expect schools to have anticipated these changes and prepared their pupils accordingly.

The study itself relies on the assumption that evidence of computer use spanning all four educational paradigms would give a strong indication that schools are preparing their pupils for the full range of computer applications in society. They describe this, if it were to be found, as the 'ideal preparation'.

With these points in mind they conclude that 'no school in the sample is currently spanning the four categories which stand as an empirical representation of ideal pupil preparation for entry to a computer-oriented world'. All applications in the sample schools were restricted to the 'instructional', 'revelatory' and 'conjectural' categories. In no case did the 'emancipatory' category apply. Having said this, the authors go further to add that 'only two schools in the sample achieve a satisfactory status by meeting, in the judgement of the authors, the requirements of the instructional, revelatory and conjectural categories.

The use of computers for control functions was particularly poor, being evident in only one school of the six, and even if we were to take the misplaced control and programming activities out of the revelatory category, putting them into the conjectural category where they belong, the picture is not significantly altered.

One striking feature which the authors do not emphasise is the obvious predominance of computer studies classes in the incidence of computer related activities in the schools. There was evidence of computers being used as teaching and learning aids in other areas, but it was sporadic and accompanied by complaints of lack of adequate facilities. Indeed the authors themselves suggest that 'the schools with better overall resource levels are spanning more of the categories of activity in the referential scheme of pupil preparation'. However, the study places rather too little emphaisis on the need for computer applications to be seen to be used appropriately across all areas of school activity, both in and out of the classroom. It seems to provide further evidence, as if it were really necessary, to support the view that our secondary schools lag far behind our primary schools when it comes to exciting and innovative uses of microcomputers across the curriculum, and hence the satisfactory preparation of the younger generation for the demands of a computer-based society.

Classifying programs by such broad functional bands as these is useful, but only in a limited way. Certainly the four paradigms help us understand something of the range of possible uses for the computer in the classroom, but on the other hand, there is an implicit assumption that a program can only operate in one mode. The truth is, of course, that many programs operate in a number of different modes depending upon what they are doing at the time. A data-base simultaneously operates in the conjectural mode, by facilitating hypothesis generation and testing, and the emancipatory mode by relieving the user of a great deal of arduous sorting of index cards. A scientific simulation simultaneously operates in the revelatory mode, by allowing the user to explore the concealed model of the process in question, and in the emancipatory mode by rapidly performing many calculations every time changes are made to the physical conditions of the experiment.

Furthermore, there is uncertainty about which mode a program is operating in if one also considers the user's intentions. When a teacher wants to quickly demonstrate a scientific principle to a whole class, using a simulation program, is it being used in the revelatory, the emancipatory or the tutorial mode? If that same teacher encourages the class to discuss and hypothesise about the possible outcomes of various changes in the input conditions, is it being used in the conjectural mode?

Gray (1984), attempts to overcome many of these problems by proposing a much simplified, though only partially successful, method of classification which owes much to a personal interest in ornithology. His aim is to suggest 'a way of looking at software which could either be part of a broader scheme or stand alone as a way of getting the feel of a piece of software and its classroom implications'. The reader is invited to imagine that, as an ornithologist in the field, there is a choice of possible telescopes which can be used to observe birds. Firstly there is the telescope having 'fixed-focus', which has been set up to look at only one bird in one place. This is rather like the 'focus' of the tutorial or drill and practice programs described earlier. Secondly, there is the telescope which has been 'pre-focused' at one distance but can swing to look at other things, to pan across the scene, allowing the user some choice. This is rather like the simulations of the 'revelatory' kind where the outcome of the exercise is relatively uncertain as the user explores the hidden model. Finally, there are the 'variable-focus' binoculars, which can be focused on anything at all just as the user chooses. This, it is claimed, is like such content free tools as word processors, data-bases and Logo. However, what the model does not take into account is that the terrain, as defined by Gray, has been fixed, and therefore the binoculars can only be focused on birds within that terrain. With a true content-free tool, the terrain itself is chosen by the user.

THE LOCUS OF CONTROL

In most suggested classification systems for educational programs there is one factor which seems to be mentioned more than any other. Who, or what, has control over the learning process. If you look back at the four paradigms, you will perhaps notice that they are arranged in a very particular order. Firstly there is the 'instructional' paradigm, in which the learner is led through a series of 'frames' or graded exercises. The program has almost complete control over the pace, and complete control over the content. Next there comes the 'revelatory' paradigm, in which the user has some control over which parts of the model are to be explored. However, the program still holds the balance of control. Finally, there are the 'conjectural' and 'emancipatory' paradigms, in which the user has a great deal of control over how the program, or 'tool', is to be used. The order in which we have looked at these four paradigms then, is determined by the locus of control, ranging from almost complete control of the learner by the program, to almost complete control of the program by the learner.

CHANDLER'S CLASSIFICATION

The concept of 'locus of control' forms the basis of a classification system (Chandler, 1984) which, in my opinion, is better than most. It fits educational programs into a number of 'models' depending upon the role played by the user. These models are arranged in a continuum as before, ranging from the locus of control being with the program, to the locus of control being with the user:

1.The Hospital Model: The user as patient.

2.The Funfair Model: The user as emulator.

3.The Drama Model: The user as role-player.

4.The Laboratory Model: User as tester.

5.The Resource Centre Model: User as artist or researcher.

6.The Workshop Model: User as inventor.

Using these models as a guide, let us take a detailed look at some examples of real programs.

THE HOSPITAL MODEL

The characteristic programs of this model, as in the case of the 'instructional paradigm', are those of the tutorial and drill and practice type. To give you a clearer idea of how these work, we will look at an example of each, and try to pick out those features which are most typical of programs of their kind.

Tutorial programs are very specific in their application, they are written to do one job, and one job only. So, rather than look at just one such program, it might be more useful to look at the facilities which can be built into any tutorial program when it has been created using a general-purpose 'authoring program'. The great advantage of authoring programs is that they can be used by anyone to create their own tutorials, suiting their own needs, without having to have any knowledge of computer programming at all. 'Author' (ESM, 1984), is one such program, specially designed for use in schools.
According to the documentation, Author offers the following features;

Use of colour graphics, coloured texts, flashing characters and double height characters which you can put exactly where you want on the screen.

Automatic scoring if you decide to create a test.

Automatic 'logging' of a student's progress through the lesson- you can look at this log and at pupil's actual responses.

Easy amending, deleting and checking facilities when, and after you have written the lesson.

Most important- AUTHOR does all of the programming for you- you simply follow the instructions and decide on the important content of the lesson.

Different Kinds of Programs

As you will remember, the distinguishing feature of a tutorial program is that the information to be presented to the learner is broken down into small steps, or 'frames'. 'Author' provides a choice of three kinds of frame, depending on what is required.

An information frame simply provides information to be learnt. Something like;

'In fourteen hundred and ninety two,

Columbus sailed the ocean blue'.

would be an information frame.

A multichoice answer frame may give information, but it always asks a question which has a number of answers. Something like this,

'In which year did Columbus set sail for America?

1. 1546
2. 1365
3. 1492
4. 1429

Choose a number and press return'.

A free format answer frame also includes a question, but this time the student must type in an answer or response. This is very useful because it can provide for a wider range of replies. For example, it might look like this;

'When Columbus sailed to America, which ocean did he cross?'

Now, there are several answers which might be acceptable that you might want the computer to count as being correct. These could include, 'The Atlantic Ocean', 'Atlantic', 'the Atlantic', 'blue', 'the ocean blue', and so on. 'Author' will accept all of these, provided they are written into the tutorial program when it is created.

When each frame is created it is a simple matter to arrange which frame or frames are to follow, this is what is known as the 'frame logic'. Frames which include a question can lead to a branch in the program so that the direction taken can depend upon the answer given. This way a correct answer can lead to the next frame in the sequence, and an incorrect answer can lead to an earlier frame for revision, or to a 'remedial loop' giving extra help with a difficult point. Of course, question frames need not require 'correct' responses, they can also be used to present options. The student can choose the area to be studied, and then follow a particular branch of the program. For example, our Columbus program might follow several themes;

'Which aspects of the voyage would you like to study next?

1. Living conditions on board ship.
2. Winds, tides and currents.
3. Navigation in the 15th Century.
4. What Columbus found when he got there.

Choose a number and press return'.

If the teacher requires, it is possible for questions to be scored, as in a test. This can be very useful sometimes to provide feedback and perhaps some added incentive to the student. But, what is perhaps more useful for the teacher, is for the students replies to be 'logged'. This means that each reply, whether right or wrong, is stored by the program and recorded onto disc for future reference. It is then an easy matter for the teacher to access that file to see just what went on during that student's session with the program. It is perhaps this diagnostic facility which teachers will find particularly attractive because it allows them to keep track of what is happening while they are elsewhere in the classroom working with other students. Sadly, many tutorial programs do not offer this facility, but, with the increasing availability of programs like 'Author', it may become more common. When we come to start thinking about software selection in chapter 4, this could well be an important feature to look out for in tutorial programs.

Drill and Practice programs are probably the most common in our schools. Unfortunately, many of them are of poor quality, but the better ones are very versatile and perform a valuable function at all levels. 'Rally' (Ladybird-Longman, 1984), is a particularly good example which is both well written and versatile. It is designed to provide opportunities to develop both speed and accuracy in computational skills over a wide range of abilities. There are, in fact, two programs, 'Rally A' and 'Rally B', offering eight levels of difficulty ranging from single digit operations at level A1, to four and five digit operations at level B4. The programs simulate a car rally in which students attempt to complete the course by answering questions of graded difficulty using the four rules of number.
    Each Rally begins with a car shown in the bottom left-hand corner of a twelve by fourteen grid. Five towns are marked on the grid, and the car is moved from point to point using the arrow keys. Although the student can choose any route to visit the five towns, an incentive to choose the shortest possible route is provided since the driver has to refuel along the way

and is also racing against the clock. Refuelling is achieved by requesting questions which must then be correctly answered. If an answer is incorrect, two further attempts are allowed before a new question appears. When the course is completed the time taken, distance travelled, remaining fuel, the number of questions answered and the number of correct answers are all displayed. Following this, a number of different options are available to the student. It is possible to try again using the same towns. This is useful if several children want to see who can cover the same course in the quickest time, or an individual child wants to improve on a previous time. A different, random, selection of towns can be chosen with the same type of questions, or questions of another kind if preferred. Of course these selections may be dictated by the teacher who wants a child to practice particular skills at a particular level. It is also suggested that teachers encourage children to record information about their games. This provides them with useful information over a period of time which could be used in learning simple statistical techniques involving mean times and distances, or the construction of bar charts and graphs. However, the record sheet also provides the teacher with a ready-made diagnostic tool.

THE FUNFAIR MODEL

It is in the funfair model that we see programs most like the arcade games which are so popular in pubs, clubs and amusement arcades. Generally, however, the speed and graphics are rather less spectacular in the microcomputer variety due to lack of memory space for such sophisticated operations. Nevertheless, the designers of these programs have been able to capture many of those aspects which make arcade games so much fun.

To present childrens' work activities in the form of games requiring quick thinking and good hand-eye coordination is nothing new. Teachers of the very young, and those having special needs have used this technique for many years. Once absorbed in playing the game, children soon forget that they must perform matching, sorting, sequencing, reading or number activities in order to achieve their objectives. Motivation is higher and concentration lasts for longer when the task is exciting, fast moving and rewarding. There is no doubt also, that a certain amount of competition can be helpful. This is perhaps where the computer can be most effective. Apart from presenting words and pictures conveniently on the television screen, it can become an opponent whose ability to play the game can be fixed by the teacher. In this way the teacher can ensure that the game is never too hard for the child to play and, for most of the time at least, to win.

Arcade games invariably involve some kind of fast moving object which has to be either guided or driven, like a car or space-craft, or it has to be captured or shot at in some way. Whichever it is, the activity requires the player or players to develop hand-eye coordination in conjunction with quick reactions using the keyboard or some other device like a joystick or concept keyboard.

'Bridge of Words' and 'Laser Letters' (Shards Software, 1983), are two good examples of this, forming part of a suite of six reading skills programs sharing a common stock of a little over 500 words. The games can be set to any one of nine difficulty levels, and in addition, the speed at which words are printed on the screen is variable. In <u>'Bridge of Words'</u> the player is invited to fill in the missing letters in words which have been arranged into the shape of a bridge. As the cursor moves along the bridge, the player has to press the key for the missing letter just as the cursor is over the place where the letter belongs in the word. If the wrong key is pressed points are lost. The cursor continues to move across the bridge, over and over again until all words are complete and the game is over. As the skill of the player increases, the speed at which the cursor moves can be increased, and more difficult words can be used to create the bridge. At the end of the game the number of tries, right answers, wrong answers and total points awarded are displayed. <u>'Laser Letters'</u> is a spelling game with a more violent theme. Using a laser gun, the player has to shoot missing letters into a moving word. The complete words are displayed first, followed by the same words with some letters missing. One of the words then moves up and down the right hand side of the screen. The player must judge when the word is in the right position before pressing the key for the missing letter. If a direct hit is scored, points are awarded. If the laser misses, points are lost and a rocket crosses the screen to destroy the laser gun. This is all accompanied by the appropriate shooting and exploding noises. The higher the level of difficulty chosen, the faster the words move. The game ends when all of the words have been completed, at which point the number of tries, hits, misses, and total points are all displayed.

THE DRAMA MODEL

The most characteristic feature of these programs is that they model some kind of world or environment for the user to explore. This usually requires the user to adopt some kind of role in order to participate in what is essentially an adventure. A famous example from the world of children's literature is 'The Hobbit' (Melbourne House, 1982), a superb adventure program to accompany Tolkein's famous book. (Tolkein, 1937). Let us look at two, contrasting programs of this kind designed for use in classrooms, 'Micro map 1 and 2' (Ladybird-Longman 1984), which is based upon an imaginary, but realistic, map of English countryside, and 'Dragon World',(4MATION 1985), which is based upon a totally imaginary and fantasy world.

'Micro map 1 and 2', centre on an imaginary village called Ferndale, and are designed to help children develop map skills in such a way that there is maximum transfer of what they learn, using the computer, to practical work in the field. For this reason the pack contains maps on various scales together with the necessary drawing and measuring instruments to enable them to use and understand paper maps. The authors (Gray and Billson, 1985), comment that:

> In our view, map skills are best acquired 'in the field' through first hand experience of a familiar locality. Consequently, we decided that our aim should be to design a resource which modelled field-work, thereby providing ready transfer of learning from a micro-world to the real environment. Such modelling would imply using a paper map since this is the form in which most people encounter maps in everyday life. Another important principle was that the program should not attempt to teach; rather it would provide a context for practising map-work skills.

Both programs use the same data-base to model Ferndale and surrounding countryside in such a way that the computer 'knows' the location of twelve named places, like 'The Old Mill', 'Swallow Cave', St. Mary's Church, and so on, and can identify and recognise thirteen kinds of terrain;

> A road
> A river
> A track
> A railway
> A village
> Farmland
> A park
> A wood
> A lake
> An orchard
> Rough grassland
> Rocky ground
> An island

all to an accuracy to the nearest degree for bearings, and to the nearest two millimetres on the map for scale distances.

Micro Map 1 provides the opportunity to explore the features of the map through four exercises; 'grid references', 'reading the features', 'scale and distance' and 'points of the compass'. These are then followed up in Micro Map 2 by more sophisticated exercises of an open-ended and interpretive kind, and the computer's answers are carefully worded to reflect the fact that there is no single correct answer to some questions:

'Which way?' to develop body orientation.
'Where are you?' for interpretation of terrain.
'As the crow flies' for interpretation of information about 'walks' across Ferndale.
'Bearings'
'Get out of that!' pin pointing your position using triangulation.

This wide range of exercises is intended to provide opportunities for experience in geographical interpretation, but it is further extended by a set of accompanying worksheets to help children think about historical and more general kinds of map interpretation. The worksheets are designed in an open-ended way to foster the drawing of parallels between Ferndale and the place where the children live.

'Dragon World' is a very different program but it does have two important things in common with 'Micro Map'. Both programs create 'micro-worlds' in which children can move about and explore, and neither program actually sets out to teach anything. As Mike Matson comments in the introduction to 'Dragon World':

No child is going to sit at a computer playing with Dragon World and come away better educated because of what he/she has seen on the screen. Dragon World was not designed to teach children anything. Its purpose was to provide a gateway to another world, a world in which children would be stimulated and motivated to ask questions, find answers, discuss issues, keep records and use their imaginations to make that world their own world. Above all, its purpose was to give teachers an opportunity to make the classroom a good place to be in.

The Dragon World adventure is in two parts, and the child must complete part one, find the five magic teeth of Bewgo, and discover the password before moving on to part two. Part one is sequential in nature, but at each stage certain tasks must be performed which make it almost impossible to find all five teeth first time around. In fact each of the tasks is designed to make children think, and to try to work out the rules which govern the task they have been set. Very often more can be learnt by getting things wrong than by finding the right answer by chance. One task is to feed a baby dragon until her weight reaches 100kg. Various foods are offered but not all are acceptable. After a while it becomes evident that it is the initial letters of the foods that are important, and that they must be offered in the sequence d-r-a-g-o-n-d-r-a and so on. Eventually the child is asked which other foods the dragon would like, and then anything can be offered provided it starts with the next letter in the sequence. When this is complete, it is followed by some dragon tricks and some dragon riddles to be solved. In the final task of part one, the child is encouraged to listen carefully to a series of musical tones. A randomly-drawn path exists across a pitch dark cave. A course must be steered through the cave using the cursor keys, the only clues to the route being a series of high and low notes to show whether one is on or near the path. If the chosen route is unsuccessful, some friendly skeletons appear and the child is invited to begin again. As the child successfully negotiates these various tasks, individual teeth are discovered.

Part two begins in a similar way to part one, but the ultimate aim is to find five 'treasures' which are to be presented to the dragons. These 'treasures', there are twenty four in all, are located in various parts of 'The town of Treasures' in which there are four territories to be explored, 'the flats', 'the tree', 'the pond' and 'the road'.

Clearly, this is a very complex program having many possible outcomes which cannot be described in a few short paragraphs. However, I hope that this description will help you get a feel for what it is trying to achieve. The program itself, like Micro Map, is accompanied by a wide range of suggestions and ideas for activities away from the computer which are appropriate to many areas of the primary school curriculum. This is often a feature of the best educational programs, something which we should bear in mind when we come to think about their selection and evaluation.

THE LABORATORY MODEL

Most laboratory simulations are of scientific processes or experiments which would otherwise be too dangerous, too expensive or too time consuming to be attempted in school. What they have in common is that they are all based upon a mathematical model of a real life situation which is unalterable. In other words the model has been fixed by the program designer in such a way that the user can only experiment with changes to those conditions which the program allows. The user plays the role of a scientist or tester who can vary a number of things in order to understand which conditions produce optimum results. There are a number of non-scientific simulations which also fit this model, things like economic simulations where various conditions like interest rates, inflation, unemployment and so on can be varied to see what would happen to the economy. Historical simulations might involve the manipulation of troop numbers and positions in a battle to see how that might have altered the outcome. Geographical simulations can build up patterns of weather conditions to see how they might affect crop yields and the demand for water supplies.

'The Manufacture of Sulphuric Acid' (Longman, 1982), is an example of a scientific simulation intended for the chemistry class. While simulating what is, commercially, a very important process, it sets out some very specific objectives;

a. to make a topic, which many students find uninteresting, a source of enthusiasm and one which will encourage them to think and participate.

b. to present information about an industrial process in such a way that the principles underlying the choice of conditions can be worked out with a consequent improvement in understanding and retention.

c. to show what is meant by 'chemical principles' and how compromise with these is almost inevitable. (p.4)

The simulation is in three parts. Part one allows the user to investigate the ways in which variations in temperature, pressure, the ratio of the basic ingredients (sulphur dioxide to oxygen), and the presence of a catalyst affect the amounts of chemicals present at equilibrium. The results can be displayed either as a table or as a graph. Each time the conditions are changed the program immediately calculates the new result. Part two enables the user to find the conditions that would produce the maximum amount of sulphuric acid in a day. Once again, the values of temperature, pressure, ratio of ingredients (sulphur dioxide to oxygen), and the presence of a catalyst can be varied and the results plotted on a graph or in a table. Part three involves the kinetics of the reaction and the concentration of the reactants, but also considers the costs involved in various stages of the process and possible pollution of the surroundings.

'Motorway Route' (Longman, 1983), is a simulation designed 'to develop an awareness of the impact of motorways upon the environment'. The authors comment that;

With all the current publicity given to environmental issues such as the siting of the third London airport, students often have a general idea of the arguments concerned with environmental planning. However, they usually have difficulty in making value judgements about the relative importance of effects upon different aspects of the environment. It is also quite difficult to convey an idea of the effect that practical and financial considerations have on environmental planning. (p.4)

The program provides the opportunity to try out alternative routes for a proposed motorway through Hatfield. The proposed routes are 'scored' by the program in a manner based upon the 'user's own subjective ideas about the impact of a motorway on various environmental factors'. The specific aims of the simulation are;

a. to develop an awareness of the scope and nature of the impact of motorways upon the environment;

b. to learn about aspects of motorway construction which are used to minimise environmental impact;

c. to provide an introduction to some of the ideas planners use to access environmental impact;

d. to develop a concept of hierarchical order in subjective assessments;

e. to provide students with an opportunity to discuss environmental planning with their peers;

f. to develop an awareness of the range of considerations involved in planning- environmental factors, cost, engineering problems. (p.5)

Although the mathematical models, upon which these simulations are based, cannot be changed by the user, they are presented and explained in detail in the documentation. This is essential if the pupil is going to fully understand how the processes work, but it is also important because it allows the teacher to judge the extent to which the models have been simplified for the purposes of clarity, and therefore to judge their accuracy.

THE RESOURCE CENTRE MODEL

The major characteristic of these programs is that they are 'content-free'. This means that they are intended to be used as tools in the classroom over a wide range of the curriculum, to store and manipulate data or information which has been supplied by the user. Some programs allow the user to create in a literary or artistic fashion, programs like word-processors and sound or graphics editors. Others allow information to be stored and investigated, like data-bases, whereas such things as scientific instruments and robots allow the user to measure and control events which are external to the computer itself.

'Edfax' (Tecmedia, 1984), is a teletext emulator which is an extremely versatile resource enabling children and teachers to create, store and display 'pages' of information, both graphics and text, which look almost identical to commercial broadcast teletext systems like Ceefax (the BBC system), and Oracle (the ITV system).

Different Kinds of Programs

This is how it is described by the authors,

> Edfax provides a simulation of teletext, except that the
> whole system resides inside your microcomputer and disc
> drive! You can create and edit your own pages of
> information and quickly display any one of up to 80 pages
> using a single 100K floppy disc drive. (p.6)

In fact Edfax is two programs, not one. The first, called
'Edit', allows the user to create pages of information on the
screen and then to save them on disc. This program is subject
to the normal restrictions of copyright. The second program,
called 'Display' enables the user to display any of the pages
which have been created and stored on the disc. This program is
not subject to copyright restrictions, and can therefore be
copied onto any disc which contains stored pages. That disc can
then be used by anyone to display pages, and it can even be
legally copied, but it cannot be used to create new pages.

The authors rightly suggest that creating Edfax pages is,
in itself, an educational experience, 'Edfax is a creative
medium and pupils can learn a good deal about, let's say,
geography, by creating teletext pages full of information
relating to various countries'. This is of course true of many
subjects, although there is more to Edfax than just storing
pages of facts to learn. The authors go on to suggest many more
educational benefits;

-language development through sentence construction,
precis, grammar, style and sequence

-synthesis, interpretation and questioning through use as
a news generator

-research through the need to check facts, spelling,
coverage, etc

-imagination, art and design, as pages are created

-overcoming writing difficulties through the creation of
clear and attractive pages

-verbal skills through group composition

-organization, planning and attention to detail as pages
are created and structured. (p.8)

Although Edfax allows for the creation and display of
'pages' of information it is not like a conventional data-base
in that it does not allow the information to be sorted and
interrogated. However, there are many data-bases available
which will do this, and no school software collection would be

complete without at least one. 'Inform' (Nottinghamshire County Council, Education Department, 1984), is one such data-base which is designed to facilitate the interrogation of fixed length record datafiles. A file is made up of related information, or data, which has been collected with a specific purpose in mind. The data that is contained in a file relates to a group of people or objects, and all information about any one of those is called a 'record'. Within each record there will be a number of individual items of information about about it, each of which is called a 'field'. For example, a file on gramophone records would contain as many 'records' as there were gramophone records in the collection. Each 'record' would contain the same items, or 'fields' of information about each gramophone record. These 'fields' might be,

1. Title
2. Artist or artist's names
3. Publisher's reference number
4. The title of each track
5. Date of publication
6. Reference number in the record collection.

Although Inform comes with a number of demonstration datafiles which are ready for study, it also provides for teachers or children to create datafiles of their own. This is a most valuable exercise for children because it facilitates the development of such a wide range of information handling skills. Files can be interrogated using Inform's sophisticated 'Find' command. This requires the user to select a 'field', specify a test to be made, and to state the value against which to make that test. For example, if we look at our file on gramophone records, we might be looking for a particular tune played by a particular artist. We could select a field- 'The title of each track', and specify a test- 'contains "I'm getting sentimental over you". We could then add 'and' 'The artist or artist's names','contains' "Roy Williams". Having done this we could specify that the following fields should be printed out, Title, Artist or artists names, Reference number in the record collection. On the command GO, the computer would search every record to see if any of them satisfied the conditions set. In our case, the result would be:

Title: Something Wonderful
Artist: Roy Williams with the Eddie Thompson Trio
Reference No: 245

So, I would need to look up a record called 'Something Wonderful', which was number 245 in my collection, and on that record I would find a track called 'I'm getting sentimental over you' played by Roy Williams.

In fact searches can become really quite complex things, including such tests as 'greater than', 'less than', 'equal to', 'not equal to', 'contains', 'does not contain', and 'starts with'. In addition such conditions as 'and' and 'or' can be added. The authors comment that in the classroom children should be encouraged to;

-formulate hypotheses based on their own previous experience or from a study of reference material:
e.g. "In the mid-1800's few people lived beyond 60 years of age"
"most pedestrian accidents involve unaccompanied children under 10 years of age".
-deduce the appropriate FIND statement to enable the required search to be carried out.
-select the data to be output when a match is found and to formulate the appropriate PRINT statement.
-carry out the search
-analyse the results and, if necessary, reformulate the original hypothesis or extend the study. (p.5)

In addition to all this, Inform allows the information to be manipulated in other ways. For example, grouped frequency distributions can be plotted, the output can be sorted into numerical or alphabetical order, or a statistical summary can be displayed.

Clearly, information retrieval provides many opportunities for children to develop a feel for information handling and to acquire the necessary skills to cope in an age where computers are becoming such common tools in both work and play. Probably the best account of work done in schools using an information retrieval package like Inform, is that by Alistair Ross (1984), and although he writes about work done with a younger age group, his discussion embodies what I consider to be the best of information handling in the classroom, and is well worthy of consideration by teachers of all age groups.

THE WORKSHOP MODEL

When discussing the use of the microcomputer as a teaching and learning aid I have emphasised that learning how to program is not an essential prerequisite. In fact it is probably true to say that, in the early days of educational computing, it was the thought of having to learn to program that put most teachers off the idea. Things are a little diferent now, of course, because newcomers can attend some good in-service courses and can also see computers being used in classrooms for a variety of purposes which do not include programming at all. Having said this, our final group of programs are in fact programming languages themselves, and although I have suggested that, for everyday use, we do not need to program, there are a few exceptions. Obviously it is essential to include programming in any course of computer studies, and although this is an important part of the school curriculum, it is rather specialised and beyond the scope of this book. It could be argued that teachers need to understand the rudiments of programming to enable them to make minor alterations to commercial programs to suit their own needs. But, if this is so important, and the program is any good, the provision for such changes should be written into the software. In other words, the program should allow for individual needs by presenting suitable options as the program is running, in what might be called a 'user friendly' way. Many children, of course, show a great deal of interest in writing programs for their home computers, and this forms a major part of the activities of many school computer clubs. This is the place for the computer enthusiasts on the school staff to participate, but it really has little to do with using computers as resources for teaching and learning during lesson times. Having said this, many teachers have been quick to recognise the enormous potential of computer programming as an intellectually stimulating exercise in its own right. In our continuum of program types, programming languages provide the user with the maximum of control over the process. By writing a program one literally tells the computer what to do. Within reason, what is possible is only limited by the programmers own imagination. To be more specific, the process of programming is thought to be an excellent vehicle for the development of skills of logical reasoning and problem-solving. Telford,(1985) comments that;

> Supporting the learning of general problem-solving skills is difficult for parents and teachers alike - indeed, it has been recognised that problem-solving is a weak spot in both adults and children across the whole country. The wide differences between various kinds of realistic problems makes it difficult for children to transfer an approach for solving one problem to another problem. There are, nevertheless, many skills that support problem-solving which are general enough to be transportable. These include the skills of:
>
> > Logic/argument
> > Reasoning/prediction
> > Ordering/sequencing
> > Hypothesising
> > Testing
> > Analysing
> > Fault-finding (debugging)
> > Design
> > Recording
> > Prototyping

If we can find a way of supporting these general skills then we are helping with general problem-solving. (p.65)

What this is all leading up to suggest is that, although many of these things could be achieved through programming in a language like Basic, it would not be without its problems, and that the alternative, and one to be much preferred, is to use Logo. There have probably been more books and papers written about Logo than about any other program or programming language within the context of education. (See Martin, 1985, as an example). As a programming language specifically for children it has no equal, and although it is best known for the facility with which children can produce intricate and appealing patterns and designs on the computer screen, called 'Turtle Graphics', Logo has much more to offer. There are, in fact, five major facilities provided by Logo which all contribute towards making it such a versatile tool. These are;

1. Turtle graphics
2. Control
3. Numerical operations
4. List processing
5. Music

They are not listed in order of importance, but in an order which perhaps reflects the degree to which they are generally known.

Turtle Graphics and Control are usually seen as being two aspects of the same thing, since control of the famous floor turtle, a dome-shaped robot, can be used to draw on paper what Turtle Graphics can do on the screen. However, this would be to ignore the wide range of other robots and devices available. Such things as cranes, robot-arms and computer controlled relays and switches can be added to the already impressive range of external devices which children can control using simple commands in Logo.

Perhaps 'simplicity' is the key word when discussing the advantages of Logo, since what all of its applications have in common is the facility to break any problem down into a series of simple operations, called procedures, which can then be strung together sequentially to perform more complex tasks. It is this process in particular which facilitates the development of Telford's (1985) list of transportable skills. This is just as true when learning how to build up a complex musical sequence, manipulate text, design custom-built numerical operations, or instruct a robot to perform a series of complex tasks. As such, Logo is a good example of a program which accords the maximum degree of control to the user. Logo, like other programming languages, is essentially a tool, a means whereby ideas and relationships can be explored, and problems can be identified, investigated and solved.

CONCLUSIONS

In this chapter I have suggested that the key to the computer's popularity is its 'versatility'. However, this, in itself, is likely to create problems for teachers who want to select or evaluate programs for classroom use. A full and detailed understanding of the variety of uses for computer software in the classroom has been suggested as an essential prerequisite for its effective selection and evaluation.

Computer programs have been classified into six types according to the role played by, and the degree of control accorded to, the user. In each case examples of programs currently in use in classrooms were used in an attempt to highlight what is the essence of each type. I have tried to suggest, by doing this, that such knowledge is important to help teachers make choices about the kind of program needed for a particular job, before deciding whether a particular program would satisfy that need.

Chapter Four

Choosing Educational Software

To decide what teachers really need to know in order to make
informed decisions about educational software is not as easy as
it may seem. There are many things which make demands on
teachers' time and which threaten to keep them out of their
classrooms. Gaining sufficient knowledge of computers and their
software is just one of many things that they must do to keep
up with developments in educational ideas and methods. Of
course, in-service courses play an important part here, trying
to acquire the necessary skills is not something which is
easily done 'on the job'. However, as we have already noted
(Jones and Preece, 1984), there is still a shortage of courses
for inexperienced teachers which satisfactorily develop these
necessary skills. If the opportunity to merely browse through
a selection of available software is insufficient, then it is
important for us to decide exactly what it is that the well
prepared teacher needs to know.

The constant need for in-service training leads to a
certain amount of conflict between time which should be spent
in the classroom or preparing and marking work, and time spent
keeping up to date with new ideas, methods and techniques. The
addition of the demands of computing to this does nothing to
make the organisation of teachers' time any easier.

It is not difficult to find examples of software which
could almost have been designed to put the newcomer off
altogether. Add this to the normal pressures of an average day
in school and one can see how easily inexperienced users can be
forced into making decisions about programs which they and
their pupils may live to regret. Busy teachers are very much in
Spielman's (1981) mind when he notes that many educational
programs;

..often display features which are distinctly uncongenial.
These usually reveal themselves by a program's capacity to
irritate or frustrate someone who tries to use or browse
through it in real workaday circumstances. The chief
sources of trouble are heavy-going admission routines,

poor presentation and layout, ungainly image movement, insecure input procedures and, in general, bad program aesthetics. (p.11)

He suggests that by making it difficult for newcomers to try them out, and by including unavoidable and wearisome rigmaroles at the beginning, followed by confusing input requirements and difficulties in correcting mistakes, all coupled with ugly presentation, is enough to annoy any teacher. This is true enough, and still all too common, but the teacher's problems do not end there. Spielman,(1982), describes what many teachers may recognise as a fairly common experience;

Typically the program comes embodied in a 'package' consisting of a disc or cassette and a dozen or so pages of print material, and it first reaches the teacher's hands at some such time as the morning break. In his hands at that moment he also has a set of papers to mark, a list of people to see, the agenda for a departmental meeting and a cup of coffee. Notwithstanding, he glances through the documentation and decides it seems interesting enough to warrant taking a look at the software in action.

Since he does not have a suitable computer at home, this will have to be fitted in during the day while he is at school. By making a special effort he manages to create a spare half hour and to persuade the computer club to allow him access to a machine.

He loads the program and gets it running. What he almost certainly does not do is sit down and read the documentation first. Indeed, it is quite likely that he has already mislaid it, but he has got a computer in front of him and, not unreasonably, he might expect sufficient guidance to be on tap from the computer itself.

What all too often happens, however, is something like this. The program starts off with an indulgent display of exhibitionism: ornate titles, animated logos, warnings against infringement of copyright, accompanied possibly by a rendering of 'I Wonder Who's Kissing Her Now?' - a pleasant diversion the first time one encounters it, perhaps, but a feature which quickly palls if it has to be endured every time the program is run.

And all this before the program itself has really started. The description continues with what Spielman calls a 'sort of obstacle course' comprising of a series of menus containing ill-defined options finally leading the poor bewildered teacher to resort to trial and error as the only way of finding out what the program is about.

Now this may sound all very amusing, and indeed some of it is just a little larger than life, but it does raise a number

of important issues which should be of interest to program
writers and users alike.

Documentation has always posed a problem. Most people seem
to be tempted to try to run a new program before they have read
the instructions. However, this usually leads to disaster with
all but the simplest of programs. There are, of course, very
good reasons why the instructions should be read first,
particularly with educational software. If one consults the
documentation one will quickly get an idea of the scope of the
program, and what the program's designer had in mind for it.
Sometimes, of course, this can be misleading since not all
program documentation is very good, some is non-existent.
There are those who would argue that information about the
program should be included within the program itself, and on
the face of it, this might seem to be a good idea. There are
problems however. If the instructions are included in the
actual program listing as REM statements (REM is a statement in
BASIC meaning 'remark'), the whole program needs to be listed
before the instructions can be read, and there really is no
justifiction for this. In any event, many programs are modified
so that they cannot be listed, as a protection against
copyright infringement. If the documentation is included as
text to be read on the screen, do we really want to see it
every time we run the program? This can be avoided by offering
the program details as a separate option so that it need only
be consulted when required, but what happens if you need to
look at them when you're half way through a tricky part of the
program run? As if these were not enough reasons for not
including the documentation in the program itself, there is yet
another more practical reason. Lengthy program notes take up a
lot of computer memory space. As programs become more and more
sophisticated, using high quality graphics and so on, memory
space is rather too precious to be used for things which are
better presented on paper anyway.

Some software authors are more understanding of these
problems than others. Indeed, some documentation is so tortuous
and complicated that its very appearance is enough to put off
all but the most determined. Fortunately this in not
universally the case. As Tony Gray, director of the
Loughborough Primary Micro Project (LPMP), recently commented
to me, 'I write this stuff in the full knowledge that no one
else is ever going to read it!' In fact, behind this apparently
jocular remark, lies a deep concern for, and understanding of
the problem, an understanding which is very much in evidence in
the LPMP program documentation itself. The program
documentation is divided into two parts. The first is
'Essential Information', which must be read in order to
understand how to get the program running, while the rest is
'The Program in Detail', which must be read later to understand
the full scope of the program and how it might be used to its
best advantage. This is made quite clear to the potential user

56

very early on so that the teacher's first experiences of the program can be as straightforward and informative as possible. Here is how it is put in the introduction to Micro Map 1 and 2, (Ladybird-Longman 1984);

> There are two ways of getting to know Micro Map 1 and 2. You can either dive into the programs, have a look and then read the rest of these notes as you need them. Or, if you prefer, you could read the detailed notes on each section commencing on page 7. In either case your work will be enhanced if you are thoroughly familiar with the programs before you take them into the classroom.
> If you want to take a quick look, read the essential information, load the program and off you go.

Titles and logos at the beginning of a program can sometimes be annoying, but one cannot blame publishers for wanting to draw our attention to their name. In some cases, however, where the program is rather long, the 'title page' can be displayed while the main body of the program is being loaded. This is an especially good idea when the program is on tape since loading a long program can be a relatively lengthy business, taking, maybe, five minutes or so. Some publishers allow the user to skip the titles simply by pressing the space bar once they have started, some of the Longman programs allow for this. Sound and music present even more problems. Far from being a welcome enhancement to educational programs, sound and music can be most unwelcome in a classroom where there are several activities going on at the same time. The best programs offer the option to either control the sound volume, like in 'Dragon World' (4MATION, 1985), for example, or to turn the sound off altogether. What we must decide in every case, of course, is whether the sound effects actually enhance the effect of the program, or whether they are an unnecessary embellishment. We will return to this problem later.

'Obstacle courses' can appear in a variety of forms, although, with the benefit of hindsight many program designers are giving this more serious attention than in the past. Programs which offer a series of menus setting out the various options available can be very useful, provided that the options are clearly stated. It is possible to suffer from 'menu overload' however, so it is important that only the essential options are presented at appropriate stages. At the same time, there needs to be the facility to allow the user to return to the main menu without having to reload and start all over again. As an alternative to the 'menu driven' program, some favour the 'command driven' style. This requires the user to learn, or have handy on a piece of paper, a whole list of commands, so that when prompted by the program, they can state their preference. This is all very well, but it does prove to be somewhat confusing to the unfamliar user, and presents a somewhat less friendly user interface than the well planned menu. If they are not familiar with how a particular set of programs are structured this presents real problems for busy teachers trying to select suitable programs for their own use. Some 'command driven' programs are so complicated that you almost need a map to find your way around them. This is particularly true of many ITMA programs with their 'drive charts', (Published by Longman), that they include a special training program called 'Testdrive' to help potential users find their way around the complicated hidden program structure.

Spielman (1981), suggests that educational programs should include what he calls a 'browse mode' especially for teachers. This would make it easier and quicker to see how the program runs, and to linger on the most interesting parts while quickly skipping over parts of less interest. Of course, some programs do already offer something similar. The teacher's notes for 'Dragon World' include a section containing the solutions to the many tasks which have to be performed. This enables the teacher to move rapidly through the program and to experiment with different solutions at any point. There is, of course, another advantage to this in that the teacher has a quick reference if a child is stuck and needs a few gentle hints as to what to try next. The disadvantage, of course, is that the notes must be kept well away from the childrens' eyes.

Some programs are accompanied by 'sample runs' printed in the documentation. These are quite useful in that it is possible to see what would happen if a particular course of action were taken, but there is no substitute for real hands-on experience.

The science simulations published by Longman include an option in the program called 'DEMO'. By selecting this option the teacher is furnished with a sample set of data which serves to illustrate how the program might be used. Starting from the data provided, individual items can be changed, one at a time, to see whether the conditions of the process or experiment can be further optimised.

WHAT TEACHERS NEED TO KNOW

In very general terms, there are four groups of really important things that teachers need to know about before they can become efficient software selectors:

1.   What you might call 'basic housekeeping'. This includes all of the day to day things a computer user must be able to do to set up the hardware, load and run programs, make back-up copies of tapes or discs, protect files from accidental erasure and so on. These are such rudimentary skills, but they are vitally important.

It is a sad fact that they are sometimes rather neglected in both initial training and in-service courses. My own experience of running such courses over a number of years is that most people need more time than one might think to come to terms with these operations so that they become 'second nature' to them. It is really not good enough to be told about them and have them demonstrated, the skills must be tried and rehearsed until the teacher is 'self-sufficient' in their use.

2.   What the range of possibilities really is for educational programs. This comes in two parts. Firstly, teachers need to have experienced the full spectrum of educational programs, from tutorials to content-free tools, with sufficient time to experiment until they can come to appreciate for themselves the educational contribution that good examples of each might make. Secondly, some experience of a programming language like LOGO to help them appreciate the potential of the hardware itself, in other words what the computer is capable of doing, and also to appreciate how versatile a learning aid a program like LOGO really is.

3.   To have a clear idea in their own minds about their curriculum objectives and the role they want the computer program to play. This can work in two ways. Firstly when a teacher is looking for a program to do a specific job, and secondly when a teacher, with general curriculum objectives in mind, is viewing a range of programs to see where some of them might perform a useful role in the already existing scheme.

4.   What makes a program a good program. Of course this issue is closely tied to the question of objectives, but there is another important element which must be considered. There are a number of things which must be looked out for which will highlight many of the technical, as well as the educational strengths and weaknesses of a program. It is these points which form the bulk of the many ill-defined 'check lists' which have been published over the years, claiming to help teachers select and evaluate programs. We will look at some of these in detail a little later in this chapter.

You may have noticed that, like Jones and Preece (1984), I have suggested some LOGO programming as a means to understanding how computer programs work and what computers can do, but I have made no mention of learning to program for its own sake. Unless a teacher is going to teach computer studies as a subject, or is enthusiastic enough to want to learn anyway, there is no justification for saying that any teacher should have to learn to program in a general purpose language such as Basic. If an educational program has been properly thought out by its authors, any changes that users might need to make should be available through the software while the program is running. Routines for editing data files are not difficult to write. Teachers' time is far too valuable to be spent tinkering around with someone else's programs when they could be preparing or marking work, or actually be engaged in face-to-face contact with children in the classroom.

CHECKLISTS AND RATING SCALES

Many so called program 'evaluations' which we see printed in computer magazines are little more than program 'reviews', descriptions of what the programs are about. These have their place, of course, but only in the sense that they draw to our attention those programs which might be worth looking at more critically. Some, however, do attempt to provide a more critical appraisal by awarding points or stars in an apparently objective sort of way. This approach creates problems of its own of course, especially since the criteria for awarding the points or stars are rarely adequately defined. So what appears, on the face of it, to be a convenient tool for standardised program evaluations, is nothing more than an invitation to make more subjective judgements.

One such scheme of 'star ratings', described by Croft and Evans (1985), was used as the basis of a software review project conducted in the Mersyside and Cheshire region of the Microelectronics Education Programme;

***** A good quality, clear, robust program of sound educational value.

**** A slick program for a run-of-the-mill idea or a program with high educational value where they could have exploited more of the computer's features.

*** Worth using with children at the price stated.

** Has programming faults or is of little educational value.

* Has programming faults and has little educational value.

NIL Probably will not RUN and would be of little value if it did.

Factors considered to provide the star ratings include presentation, educational value, robustness, use of computer's facilities, quality of support materials or documentation and cost.

The authors suggest that the system was introduced to guide teachers to 'take a second look' at programs that could be interesting. If one considers the ill-defined criteria listed above, it would be, to say the least, arrogant and presumptuous to suggest anything else. Surely such judgements as 'sound educational value', 'quality' and 'worth using' can only be made in the context of the purpose the potential user has in mind for the program.

A rating-scale of points from one to five is suggested by Mullan (1982), having fifteen criteria in all, grouped under four headings;

1. 'Aims'. Concerned with program objectives, quality of presentation, information about the program and the validity of its content.

2. 'With regard to the program itself'. Concerned with its robustness and ease of use.

3. 'Documentation'. Concerned with presentation, packaging and level of helpfulness.

4. 'Children's reactions'. This is a little out of place here since headings one to three are concerned with pre-classroom selection activities, whereas number four cannot be considered until the program has been purchased and used in the classroom for some time. However, credit must be given for the suggestion that the childrens' reactions might be considered at all.

A similar idea was adopted by the magazine 'Personal Computing Today' for all their software reviews. (see p.57, May 1984). The suggested headings are;

1. Program quality

2. Crashproofing

3. Value for money

4. Ease of use

5. Supplied instructions

6. Presentation on the screen.
   (used in an earlier edition, November 1983)

Apart from using similar criteria for rating, these schemes share the same total lack of guidance for the user. Not only do they never satisfactorily explain to the novice what the individual criteria mean, but there is never any suggestion as to what might constitute good or bad examples of each.

An alternative to star and number ratings is, of course, a verbal description of the strengths and weaknesses of the program. Very often the problem with these is that little guidance is given to help teachers write their own or to interpret other people's. Here is one example (Fisher, 1983), which is intended as advice for newcomers;

How to recognize a good program

Obviously the more programs a teacher sees, the easier it will be to sort out the wheat from the chaff. However, for newcomers, the main questions to ask are: does this offer a child new educational experiences; is it relevant to your age group; will it help to develop skills; will a child be able to understand the program and respond to it; and will a child be interested enough to develop the work?

All resonably sound advice you might think. However, not only are the suggested questions ill-defined, but it is difficult to judge whether children will respond to a program unless you already have considerable experience of using programs in the classroom already. In any event, it does not differentiate between positive and negative responses, and no mention is made of the teacher's own objectives or intentions at all.

There are, of course, any number of more comprehensive check lists which are intended to help teachers produce some sort of assessment profile of a program. The magazine 'Primary Teaching and Micros' uses the following headings to describe 'software received';

Name
Publisher
Format. eg tape/disc
Price
System
Level (age)
Program type
Graphics
Sound
Options
Documentation
Packaging
Overall comments
Conclusions

These headings are simply used as a basis for a straight description of the program, and as such, can provide enough information to help teachers decide whether the program is worth looking at in action. What it does not do is to provide a satisfactory evaluation which would be sufficient to help a teacher decide whether to buy or not. In the January 1984 issue of the same magazine there are a suggested 'Eight Steps to Evaluation';

1. Package title, source, machine, memory size, special equipment required.

2. Subject area, topic, target age, target ability, class, group or individual use.

3. Brief description.

4. Definition of educational aims and objectives.

5. Appropriate use of sound, colour, graphics.

6. Documentation, screen instructions, user adaptable?, ease of use.

7. Achievement of educational objectives, robustness, educational value.

8. Technique used, what sort of program is it?

Here we have a list of important things to look out for, although, once again, little help is given in coming to terms with why some of the things listed are so important. However, the eight steps are intended for use by individual teachers to help them look more closely at programs in a more systematic way. The editorial staff of the magazine suggest that teachers might make photocopies of the list and use it in schools and teachers' centres. Finally they invite comments from the teachers who have used it. All good stuff if it serves to encourage teachers to think about the usefulness of such an instrument, and to stimulate some kind of dialogue. After all, the very act of trying to use it while experimenting with programs should go some way towards providing the necessary experience to make the teacher a better program assessor in the future. The important thing is to remember that these check lists have their limitations, but that, at the same time, they can provide an all important framework within which the software reviewer can work. Eric Deeson (Deeson, 1983), summed up the feelings of many computer users when he wrote;

> I admit that being a scientist, I went through a phase of dreaming that one could quantify the items in the list in such a way as to produce a detailed profile of the effectiveness of a program. But of course that is a dream! A given program can be highly effective with one class and quite useless with another. All sorts of practical factors intrude into the concept of objective assessment.

> So the dream has faded.
> All the same, a list of points to bear in mind when assessing software is not, I hope, entirely useless. Certainly I find that, as a reviewer or as an assessor, I now automatically and rapidly run through such a mental check-list in order to produce a judgement like this - 'could be good with fairly intelligent fourth-years who've done some work on grommets; awful grammar; unthinking use of colour and sound; inadequate help facilities; pacing needs improvement in section 3'. (p.117)

Here Deeson is suggesting that he has become so familiar with his preferred check-list, that it has become second-nature to him. He doesn't need to refer to it every time because its categories automatically come to mind every time he looks at a program. This desirable state is one which can only be achieved through practice and experience. The more you use your check-list the easier it becomes.

So what might one realistically expect from using any reasonable check-list? Anita Straker, (Straker, 1982), suggests that check-lists should be able to help you provide the answers to three major questions about any educational computer program;

1. What kind of program is it?

2. Is it in principle suitable for the general teaching scheme of which it would be a part?

3. What are its merits and in what ways could it be improved?

Note here that Straker draws our attention to the importance of considering the teacher's intentions and the need for the program to fit into the existing or proposed curriculum model.

MODIFYING PROGRAMS

So far I have made a point of emphasising that there is no justification for saying that teachers, as computer users, should be able to write or modify programs. In my experience of organising and teaching on 'computer awareness' courses, if there has been one thing causing apprehension in the minds of many teachers, it has been the prospect of 'having' to learn programming. There is no more justification for knowing how to modify a computer program than for knowing how a video recorder stores moving pictures on a length of flimsy tape. Both the computer and the video recorder are primarily resources to be used just like any other educational resource. Having said this, of course, there will always be those enthusiasts who will want to tinker with program code, and I would not want to suggest that they should leave well alone. However, it is important to realise that they do this as 'computer enthusiasts', hopefully in their spare time, and that it is by no means a requirement of all computer users.

Some check-lists include a section relating directly to the modification of program code, but really, if one knows enough about programming to be able to do it, one hardly needs to be reminded of what to look for. If, however, one does not, then the mere suggestion that the program code should be listed and inspected makes little sense and is likely to prove both confusing and off-putting. One such example, (Nash and Ball, 1982), lists eight points;

program code

Is it clear?
Is it modular?
Is it readable?
Are identifiers (names of modules and of variables) chosen to reflect their purposes?
Are errors trapped to your satisfaction?
Does it use special language features? If so
have you got these?
Can you alter it if you wish?
Can you develop it if you wish?

Now, apart from the question of 'error trapping', which we will consider later in this chapter, there is little that the non-expert can do with a check-list of this kind. The best advice one can offer is to suggest that for all practical purposes this section is unimportant and can therefore be safely ignored, or, use a different check-list.

Sensibly, Ian Brown (Brown, 1984), keeps his suggestions for program modification quite separate, while his check-list concentrates, for the most part, on educational rather than computing issues. Nevertheless, there are a few technical points to be taken into account;

Technical
Is the program available on either disc or cassette as required?

Will the program run on my particular make and model of machine with my operating system and version of Basic?

Is a printer needed?

These are all very rudimentary technical points which can be answered by reference to the program documentation and the publisher's advertising material. None of them is beyond the capabilities of a teacher who can cope with the 'basic house-keeping skills' mentioned earlier in this chapter.

This is then followed by points which relate specifically to ways in which the program might be used as a teaching and learning resource;

Educational
Is the program the best way of teaching the topic?

Are there more efficient cheaper methods?

Is the teaching method educationally sound and appropriate for the age and ability group for which it is intended?

Does it lead on to other programs in a series?

Is it consistent with the approach of other programs being used, or will its terminology and notation cause confusion?

Is it compatible with teaching methods in general use in the school?

Does the program relate positively to other classroom activities, or is the use of the microcomputer a completely unrelated activity?

Does the program keep a record of the child's results?

Is there any evidence that the program has been well tried and tested in schools?

Were class teachers involved in a feed-back process at the design stage?

Practical
Is the package easy to use?

How much time must the teacher spend selecting skill-level, number of questions, etc, before the child can begin?

Is the supporting documentation adequate and clear?

Is the program child-proof?

Does the program progress at the right speed for the child?

These final, practical points, still relate to teaching, but more from a management point of view.

Brown's suggestions for possible program modifications need not concern us here since they really are the province of the programming enthusiast. However, as a word of warning, he very sensibly suggests that if you intend to make changes to commercially written software, you should, for reasons of copyright, note that you have done so at the beginning of the program code.

Before we move on to look at some selection criteria in more detail it might prove helpful if we were to summarise what appear to be the major strengths and weaknesses of assessment check-lists.

Strengths

1. Check-lists provide a systematic framework within which assessments can be made. By using a check-list the teacher can be sure that none of the important points have been forgotten.

2. Check-lists are particularly useful as an aid to selecting software outside of the classroom.

3. Check-lists are easy to learn, and are relatively quick to apply. This, of course, presupposes that the teacher fully understands the meaning and importance of each of the criteria included in the list.

4. With practice the check-list can become second-nature to the user.

Weaknesses

1. Check-lists can be confusing if the assessment criteria are not adequately explained.

2. Check-lists can be off-putting to the newcomer if they suggest listing and inspecting program code.

3. Check-lists are less objective than they might at first appear. Judgments which users make about programs, even if they award stars or points, are subjective, being based upon their own past experiences and expectations for the future. Check-lists should always be used with particular children and/or a particular curriculum model in mind.

4. Check-lists cannot be used to quantify a program's worth.

5. Check-lists generally do not help in the evaluation of software in use in the classroom.

Choosing Educational Software

TESTING A CHECKLIST

It is not often that one gets the opportunity to test the
effectiveness of a check-list. In any event it is not something
that the individual teacher might want or even need to do.
Preece and Jones (1985), describe an experiment designed to
test the effectiveness of the 50 hour Open University
in-service training course P541, called 'Micros in Schools:
Educational Software'. (Open University Press, 1984). The
course is designed to provide teachers with enough information
and experience to be able to confidently assess educational
computer software using a purpose-built check-list. The course
itself contains all of those elements which we have already
discussed as being essential to the acquisition of necessary
skills for effective program assessment. Briefly, what they did
was to teach the course in the normal way to a group of
eighteen practising teachers, eleven from secondary schools,
five from primary schools and two from special schools. Half of
the teachers had some programming experience in Basic and they
had all used microcomputers to the extent that some had even
had some classroom experience with one of the test programs.
Towards the end of the course the teachers were shown case
studies of the programs, followed by the programs themselves to
be studied and assessed using the standard assessment criteria.
The selection criteria used were arranged into six sections,
and the users were invited to rate each on a semantic scale
from one to five as well as to write verbal comments beside
each one. The selection sheet provided also included a box
labelled 'not applicable'.

Software selection criteria

1. Educational Documentation

      1a. Statement of aims and objectives
      1b. Information about the content and background
      1c. Statement of intended type of use and audience
      1d. Suggestion of ways to use the program
      1e. Pupils activities or worksheets
      1f. Instructions for running the program
      1g. Presentation of a typical run
      1h. General impressions

2. Achievement of Stated Aims
(as far as you can tell without actually using the
program)

      2a. Aims/objectives
      2b. General impressions

3. Appropriateness of the Micro and Program

3a. For teaching this topic
3b. For the suggested audience and type of use
3c. General impressions

4. Screen Presentation

4a. Use of graphics
4b. Use of colour and animation
4c. General impressions

5. Friendliness and Flexibility of the Program

5a. Helpful messages to correct user errors
5b. Help to pupils in understanding the program
5c. Versatility so that the user can control what the program does
5d. Feedback to pupils
5e. Program adapts to pupils' performance
5f. Record of pupils' performance kept by program
5g. Program model accessible to pupil
5h. Suggestions or help for teacher to modify the program
5i. General impressions

6. Technical Documentation

6a. Information about machine requirements
6b. Information about the model used
6c. Information about the program structure
6d. Listing and readability of the program code
6e. Portability, ie. ability to transfer program to a different computer
6f. General impressions

(pp.14-15)

The teachers' summary scores for each section were then combined to produce an 'average summary rating' for each of the three programs.

From our point of view the actual values of the average summary ratings are not important, in fact I have already suggested that the quantification of a program's worth is not possible. However, what Preece and Jones are doing here is to attempt to produce a crude measure of the relative quality of one program against another. So, what might happen, then, if we tried the exercise for a second time with a different group of teachers? Would the results be comparable?

A SECOND EXPERIMENT

In the same year I conducted a similar experiment at
Loughborough University using the same selection criteria,
following a course of similar length and having similar
content. Although it was appreciated that the courses were
slightly different, and so any strict statistical analysis
would be impossible, it was felt that the similarities were so
great that a comparison of results from both experiments should
at least bring to light some important principles concerning
the validity of check-lists in general, and of this one in
particular. This time there were fifteen teachers, some from
secondary schools and some from primary schools. None of them
had any programming experience except for their contact with
Logo whilst on the course, and for several of them, this was
their first contact with a microcomputer. Unfortunately, the
teaching pack kindly lent to us by the Open University's
Nottingham office contained only two of the original three
programs assessed by Preece and Jones' group, so although three
programs were used on the second occasion, I will only discuss
the results obtained from those two. The two programs were
'Climate', produced by Fiveways (Heinemann, 1981), a
drill-and-practice program designed to reinforce the
understanding of climate types, and 'Pirates', produced by the
ITMA team (Longman, 1981), which is a treasure-hunt game for
use by the teacher with a whole class to develop skills in the
use of two and three dimensional coordinates. To my mind both
programs are getting a little long in the tooth and are not the
best examples to be chosen for such an exercise. However, it
was important to keep as many of the conditions the same as
possible in both exercises. Once again, after the teachers had
read the case studies and tried out the programs they used the
software selection criteria to assess them. The average summary
ratings were then calculated in exactly the same way as before.

Table 5.1: Comparison of average summary ratings for two
programs.

Criteria	Climate Ex.1	Ex.2	Pirates Ex.1	Ex.2
Educational documentation	3.5	3.2	4.5	3.4
Achievement of stated aims	3.5	3.4	4.9	3.2
Appropriateness of the media and the program	3.0	4.0	4.2	3.6
Screen presentation	3.7	2.6	3.8	2.0
Friendliness and flexibility	3.0	2.6	3.4	2.5
Technical documentation	2.8	2.4	3.8	3.2

Although one might not expect the two groups of scores to agree exactly, it might be reasonable to expect that the pattern of scores might be similar as one goes down the lists. If they were, we might be able to say that, although the numerical scores themselves are of little meaning, the check-list itself appears to be fairly consistent when it is used by different groups of teachers looking at the same programs. If this were the case then it would suggest that perhaps other people's assessments could function as a reliable guide for those who read them. Now of course we must accept that the sample size in this experiment is small, and that the two courses, though very similar, were not the same. However a simple non-parametric test of correlation, (the Pearson Product Moment Correlation Coefficient), between the average summary ratings of the two exercises, for both programs, revealed absolutely no statistically significant association between the two sets of ratings whatsoever. This would seem to further suggest that the numerical scores are quite arbitrary, being subject to the individual teacher's past experience and very personal ideas about what could be done using that program with a particular class. Remember that the teachers in the first experiment had all had some previous computing experience, and some had actually used 'Pirates' in their own classrooms. This probably accounts for the higher ratings awarded to 'Pirates' by that group, since they were likely to be looking at it in the light of very specific classroom experience, rather than as newcomers. It just happens that 'Pirates' is a program which performs better in the classroom than one might expect from just looking at its rather unimaginative screen display. Furthermore, the difference between the mean scores awarded by the two groups to 'Pirates', but not to 'Climate', was highly significant (t=3.353, significant at the 0.005 level), adding further weight to the argument. In the case of 'Climate', niether group had had any previous experience of the program.

What was particularly interesting, however, was the striking similarity between the written comments about the two programs made by the two groups of teachers. In the case of 'Pirates', most agreed that the program was 'very appropriate for the medium, but not well exploited', being particularly critical of the unimaginative screen display. However, the teachers who had not experienced the program in the classroom displayed less enthusiasm for the ITMA 'command driven' style of program design. In the case of 'climate' the similarities were equally as striking, particularly with regard to the inadequate definition of categories and the inaccurate information given. This finally came to a head when the program proclaimed that 'China' could represent just one climatic type, and when 'Great Britain', as a climatic type, consistently turned up in the southern hemisphere. Finally, and not related to the content of either program, the teachers in the second group, having had no previous programming experience, commented that they were confused and put off by the criteria in the check-list which related to the listing and portability of program code (criteria 6c, d and e).

So, what can we learn from the comparison of these two experiments? There seem to be four major points;

1. Beware of numerical and star ratings, they are not as objective as they may appear.

2. Written or verbal descriptions and comments are probably more reliable as a general guide.

3. Remember that your selection, and that of others, depends on what you, or they intend doing with the program. The decisions you make about its suitability or 'worth' depend a great deal on your past experience, not just as a computer user, but as a teacher as well. You must also bear this in mind when you read other people's assessments, especially if you do not know who they are and how they work.

4. Listing and modifying code isn't important and shouldn't be necessary.

Very similar conclusions were reached by Chambers and Sprecher (1983), when they wrote:

> 'A checklist is a useful tool in ensuring that all issues are addressed and that multiple evaluations are somewhat comparable. The checklist is, however, only a tool, and the heart of the evaluation should be formed by the professional training and experience of the evaluator. We therefore recommend in favour of subjective ratings and against quantitative approaches where the overall evaluation is projected by a mathematical treatment of individual ratings'. (p.71)

FROM WEAKNESS TO STRENGTH

From our list of weaknesses of check-lists as a guide to program selection, there are two which seem to contribute most to the confusion of potential users;

1. The selection criteria are generally inadequately defined or explained.

2. There are almost always some selection criteria which are inappropriate to the program being studied. This is because most check-lists are designed to suit all purposes, and ignore the need to consider the more specialised strengths and weaknesses of different kinds

of programs. There are specific things that we need to know about drill and practice programs which do not apply to simulations, information retrieval packages need to be assessed in a different way to adventure games, and so on.

These weaknesses are further highlighted by Chambers and Sprecher (1983), when they comment that:

'Since the checklist assists the evaluator in a qualitative judgment about the degree to which the courseware will contribute towards a pedagogical objective, it is not critical that individual criteria be mutually exclusive nor that in total they all be given equal weight. Different criteria are appropriate for different educational settings and instructional strategies. Few criteria are mandatory in that they alone represent a go-no go decision...... Therefore different criteria or possibly even different checklists altogether may be developed for different strategies or educational settings'. (p.71)

In attempting to come to terms with these weaknesses we need to look at, and explain in detail, those assessment criteria which might apply to all kinds of educational programs irrespective of their function, and then to consider separately those which pertain more specifically to tutorials, games, simulation games, experimental simulations, content-free tools and programming languages respectively.

GENERAL SELECTION CRITERIA

At this point it would be very tempting to try to produce yet another 'original' check-list to add to the already numerous examples available in the literature. However, what seems more sensible is to take the most commonly occurring criteria from a few of the better ones, and to look at them in detail. After all, not everyone will favour the same list, and in this way we can probably cover a wider range of possibilities. The main headings which I shall use for these general criteria are arranged roughly in the order that a teacher might be expected to want to consider them. However, this does not mean that they need necessarily be taken in that order;

1. Documentation. (i) Technical. (ii) Program information.
2. Presentation and layout.
3. Friendliness and flexibility.
4. Achievement of stated aims.
5. Robustness.

If, at this stage, you feel that there are things which have been left out, remember that they are quite likely to appear later as specific criteria for one or more of the six program types mentioned above.

1. DOCUMENTATION: (i) Technical

   a. Does the program have any accompanying documentation?

This may seem to be rather an obvious question to ask, and in fact it does seem to crop up quite regularly. Of course, it is important to know the answer to this question, but in most cases no indication is given as to whether it is necessarily a good thing or not. If you read the documentation first it can save you a great deal of time, but as I have mentioned before, there is always a great temptation to try the program first and then to refer to the instructions when you get stuck. Good documentation will start by setting out clearly, and in simple terms, what sort of computer the program is written for and what special features it may require, eg. high resolution graphics, colour, a particular size of memory expressed in units called 'K', ie. 16K, 32K, 64K and so on. Next it should give you a set of simple instructions on how to get the program running before going into a detailed discussion of its finer points. Sometimes these points are covered by separate questions like;

   b. Are there any simple loading and running instructions?

This is important, to save you time, but if there do not appear to be any you can still get by. Most software publishers adopt a standard loading and running procedure for all their programs. So, if you have used one, you can probably get into any of the others by using the same method. if in doubt, you should always try the simplest method first, which is recommended by the computer manufacturer in your user's handbook.

   c. Does the program require anything other than the most elementary knowledge of the computer to get it up and running?

It should not be necessary to be a computer expert in order to use it as a teaching and learning resource in the classroom. If you are invited to type in all sorts of strange things before the program will work, it probably means that the program has not been thoroughly planned and thought out. Take care, it could mean that other parts of the program design, which are less visible, leave something to be desired. A really good program, in this context, is one which will load and run automatically following one simple command, or even better, at the press of a key.

d. Are hardware requirements made explicit in the simplest of terms?

Once again the question of 'expertise' arises here. The information you require should be readily available in the User's Handbook. If not, then you may need to seek the advice of a colleague, or the person who supplied the computer. Once you have the information, it would be as well to write it on a sticky label and attach it to the computer or the monitor for future reference. At some stage or other you may need to know about some of the following;

i. Memory size, expressed in multiples of 'K', eg. 16K, 32K etc. The higher the number, the bigger the memory. Longer and more sophisticated programs generally require more memory.

ii. Version of BASIC. eg, Basic 2, or RML BASICSG, and so on.

iii. Operating system version number. The operating system of a computer gets things organised so that the computer can follow the instructions contained in your program. e.g. OS.1.2, or CPM 1.4, etc.

iv. Does it have a disc filing system (DFS)? All microcomputers that you will come across in school will be able to load and save programs using tape cassette, but not all of them are equipped to use a disc drive.

v. Does the computer have a network filing system (NFS)? Some computers can be connected together in a 'network' so that they can all be controlled centrally, using one disc drive and printer etc. You need to know if your computer is a part of such a network. Sometimes a computer which is equipped to be a part of such a network, but is not connected to one, can experience certain problems with some programs. If this occurs you may need to seek expert advice.

vi. What kind of graphics facility does your computer have? Is it High Resolution (HRG), Medium Resolution (MRG), or Low Resolution (LRG)? The higher the resolution the finer the detail that can be drawn on the screen, but at a price. The better the graphics, the more memory space it occupies.

vii. Does it have a facility for sound? Also, it will not be long before you will need to know whether it has a facility for speech, and if so, which system does it employ?

viii. Is your computer display in colour or black and white?

I have deliberately not referred to particular makes of computer here because there are so many varieties. However, I hope that you have now got some idea of what to look out for. It is probably a good idea to collect together all of this information before you start trying to assess programs. Attach one copy to your computer, and keep another copy with you for when you visit your teachers' centre or software supplier. If you do this it won't be long before you don't need to refer to it because you will have remembered it.

e. Are instructions given for making a back-up copy of the tape or disc? If not, do the publishers offer a replacement service for corrupted discs and tapes?

Some publishers urge you to make a back-up copy before you use the program, allowing you to keep the original safely locked away. This is a good idea because you can always prepare a fresh back-up copy if the first one becomes damaged, saving time and inconvenience. However, some publishers, being so anxious about software piracy and copyright, protect their programs in such a way that they are very difficult to copy. If they do this, then they should make it very clear in the documentation how you should go about obtaining a replacement. However, remember that you have already paid for the program once, and so the cost of a replacement should be little more than the cost of a blank disc or cassette.

f. Does the documentation include a list of other machines for which a version of the program is available?

This can save you a great deal of time, especially if you can only view a version intended for a different machine from your own. If your computer is included in the list, you will be pretty safe in ordering the right version.

DOCUMENTATION: (ii). Program information

a. Are the aims and objectives of the program made clear?

It is very important that you should be able to find this out easily before you make any serious attempts to judge the suitability of the program. Unless you know what the designer had in mind for the program, it will be very difficult to assess whether it may or may not fulfil those objectives if used with the class you have in mind. However, sometimes the objectives of a program are deliberately left vague. This is done to enable the user to adapt more readily to the needs of the curriculum. This is perfectly acceptable, provided that is made clear in the documentation, and you realise that assessing the suitability of the program will take you somewhat longer as you come to consider how you might use it to its best advantage. Beware, however, this does not apply to all programs, especially those which have been written by amateurs who may not have considered the question of objectives at all.

b. Does it specify the age and ability range for which it was designed? What degree of flexibility does it provide?

Sometimes it is quite difficult to decide which age groups would benefit from a program until you have spent some time trying it out. It is a great help if the documentation includes some discussion of this together with the results of any school trials which might help you to make a decision. Some programs have a very specific target age and ability group, these are the ones you must be most careful about. Some tutorial and drill programs may depend very much upon the users having covered certain skills to a certain level. Laboratory simulations generally require the user to have at least grasped the basic principles of the process or experiment before exploring it further. You also need to know something about the difficulty of the concepts involved, something which might appear in the detailed discussion of the program content. However, it is not only content which is important. You need to know whether the style and complexity of the language used on the screen is at a level with which your class will be happy and can cope.

More flexible programs will cater for a wider age and ability range, and you may feel that they are somewhat better value for money, having a wider range of use in the school. This can be best illustrated with drill and practice programs like 'Rally' (Longman 1984) described earlier, and a programming language like LOGO.

c. What kind of program is it?

By this time you may already have come to some conclusions about this, since it may be quite implicit in the statement of aims and objectives. However, this is not always as clear as it might be, and if the author has taken the trouble to discuss the program type in the documentation there is a reasonable chance that some thought has been given to the underlying perspective on learning. However, take care as this may not always be the case. Some discussion of the program type may give you valuable clues as to how the author sees the program being used in the classroom, whether it is intended for use with a whole class, a small group or individually. Of course, you will have the final say here in the light of your own experience as a teacher, but if the author has included results of trials carried out in schools it will give you much more to go on.

> d. Does the program allow for any alterations to be made? If so, are the instructions unambiguous and easy for the non-expert to follow?

I include this one while having certain reservations about it. I have already discussed the disadvantages of suggesting that teachers should be able to modify programs to suit their own needs. However there are some programs which allow the user to do this simply through a list of options, these I think are probably the best, and there are others which invite you to 'tinker with the code'. This is not uncommon with some laboratory simulations where Data can be modified to suit local conditions. If the instructions are clear about how to list the program and which lines to change, it can be reasonably straightforward if you are not easily put off by what you see on the screen. As I have remarked before, there is no real reason these days why this should be necessary at all since Data can be easily handled as data-files which could be changed using a 'Change Data' option in the program. Probably the best advice for the newcomer to these things is 'if in doubt, then leave well alone'.

> e. Does the documentation contain instructions for a 'browse mode' or details of a 'sample run'?

Very often it is helpful to see what would happen at various points in the program without having to work all the way through it. Some programs allow this by either giving special instructions for the teacher to 'browse', or alternatively, the documentation contains a printout of a sample-run to illustrate how the program works. This is by far the commonest way, often being broken down into sections accompanied by some detailed explanation, and some suggestions of how that part of the program might be used.

You might also expect to find a discussion of any unusual features in the program, things which you might not normally expect. Kleinman, Humphrey and van Buskirk (1982), raise an interesting issue here when discussing drill and practice programs involving addition:

> Most addition programs provide examples of programmers' failure to adapt the computer to the user. When children do addition problems with paper and pencil the addends

are usually written one below the other, with the columns in line. The children work the problem from right to left, and mark carying from one column at the top of the next. Many addition programs present the addends side by side, require the answers to be entered from left to right, and do not provide any way of marking carrying. In using these programs, children often copy the problem, work it on paper, and then enter their answer into the computer. Programs that present problems this way force the user to adapt to the computer. With more effort on the part of the programmer, the computer could have been adapted to the user.

The trouble with this is that, if the program has been properly planned and designed, the programmer would have had no say in how the working was to be presented on the screen anyway, the programmer should just write the code. However, what is more important is that they seem to be unaware of the possibility that a program designer may want to allow the teacher to deliberately force the child into working in a particular way. There are times when pencil and paper tasks are important, and the computer can be used to force children to do them quickly and accurately. This is not unique to computers; surely teachers do this all the time by organising exercises and activities in such a way as to force their children to look at a problem from a different perspective. Perhaps the best thing to do is to offer teachers the choice, in this instance, of which way the sums are to be presented on the screen. After all, this is an educational decision to be made by the teacher who is going to use the program, a decision to be based upon experience and professional judgement.

If a 'browse' option or a sample run are missing from the documentation, it might be inconvenient, but it should not affect your decision about the suitability of the program itself.

2. PRESENTATION AND LAYOUT

Here, we are particularly interested to see that text, graphics and sound have been used to their best advantage. Try to adopt the same critical eye that you use when reviewing and selecting text or library books for your class or school. Your own professional judgment is just as important here as when you plan a blackboard or transparency layout or when you prepare a worksheet or class handout.

Text.

a. Are instructions clear and unambiguous?

Writing instructions which are unambiguous and easy to follow is sometimes more difficult than it sounds. You can never be sure that the reader is going to see the problem from the same angle as you do, or that the style and complexity of language with which you are comfortable will necessarily be understood by others. This is a common problem faced by teachers, and it is always important to ensure that the children can cope with the language, both written and spoken, which they encounter during the course of their studies. This is a particular problem with computer programs because, to avoid constant repetition, instructions may be abbreviated or replaced by a symbol. This is further complicated because it is quite rare to be able to browse through the program or to return briefly to the beginning to have another look at the instructions without having to start all over again. Where instructions do appear on the screen they should be in a prominent enough place not to be missed, but at the same time they ought not to detract from the activity in hand. Any text which appears in the top or bottom left hand corners of the screen probably means that the program designer has not given it much thought, since this is where the computer will automatically print it in the absense of any other instructions.

Where instructions are not printed in full, it should be obvious what the child is expected to do. The classic examples of where this is a problem is in many arcade-type games where the instructions are briefly displayed at the beginning, but are inaccessible during the program run. In the case of 'command driven' programs, for example, all commands must be readily to hand in a list which the child can have by the computer. Also it should be possible to list them on the screen without disturbing the program run. This is usually done by including a command like 'HELP' or 'COMMANDS', which produces the list on the screen, followed by an invitation to choose a command from the list. Where instructions are abbreviated, their full meaning should be obvious, not just to you, but to the children in the ability range that you have in mind. When symbols are used, their meaning should appear all together on one convenient page in the program documentation so that they are available for easy reference. It is important to you, when you try the program for the first time, that this information is contained in the initial instructions for getting the program going. As children use the program, they should find that they come to learn what the symbols mean and so do not have to refer to the instructions. For this reason it is important for you to ensure that the use of symbols is consistent, that they always mean the same thing, and that they always appear in the same place. A very good example of this can be found in the programs of the Loughborough Primary Micro Project (LPMP, published by Ladybird-Longman), where a coloured rectangle in the corner of the screen means 'press the space bar', and a different coloured text is used to denote that input is required from the keyboard. The full explanation of the instructions is prominently displayed in the documentation and is expressed in simple language.

b. Is each frame attractively presented avoiding irrelevant detail?

Screen layout is of paramount importance. You should be able to expect that each screen display has been carefully planned to have the maximum effect. This is just as important for the positioning of text as it is for diagrams and pictures. One of the worst faults, which was sadly all too common in the early days, is for text simply to scroll up the screen as the program progresses. There is only one kind of program where that is acceptable, and that is with a word processor, where the user should be able to scroll up and down the screen at will.

c. Have coloured and double height characters been used to their best advantage?

Very often coloured text can be used to enhance or to accentuate a point, but the careless choice of colours can cause problems. Sometimes this just means that the result is unattractive, the colours clash or tend to merge making it difficult to read the words. More seriously, however, you should make sure that the choice of colours will not create problems for sufferers from colour blindness, especially the red-green form, which is a sex-linked character, being transmitted from women to their sons, and therefore much more common in boys. So, beware of combinations of shades of red and green in particular, since the problem is probably more common than you think. Children are very good at finding ways of hiding disabilities of this kind. I have a friend who drove a fire engine for years before they discovered that he suffered from red-green colour blindness. He used to respond to traffic lights by noting which lamp was alight, not by its colour. Unfortunately a computer display provides insufficient information to allow for colour blind children to compensate in this way.

Not all computers can conveniently produce double height characters, but most can be programmed to make large characters using their graphics facility. There are many occasions when this is advantageous, especially in programs designed for young children or for those with sight or perceptual problems.

Graphics.

d. Is the use of graphics appropriate to the aims and objectives of the program?

You can approach this one in a number of ways.

Particularly you will want to consider whether your aims and objectives differ in any way from those stated by the program designer. If they do, it could be that the graphics are too childish or too adult for your group;

>   i. Is the style of graphics suitable for the age and ability group you have in mind?
>
>   ii. Do the graphics serve to clarify or enhance the points being made?
>
>   iii. If there are no graphics, would the program have been improved by their inclusion?

Point (iii) is one that you can't really do much about, except write to the author with your suggestions for a revised version, or, more seriously, to produce diagrams or charts of your own to be used alongside the program if you think it is worth it. If you choose to do this, it can transform a mediocre program into a resource which, amongst others, might do a creditable job.

>   e. If pictures and diagrams are included, could they be represented more effectively by some other means? e.g. a printed sheet, a map or a photograph.

Sometimes, of course, the quality of the graphics is less important than the point being made. This may be especially true when the graphics are included to create atmosphere or simply to provide some variety to the visual effect, 'Granny's Garden (4MATION, 1984), and 'Dragon World' (4MATION, 1985) are good examples of this. However, on other occasions the quality of the picture is all important, and in some cases it might be that the microcomputer is just not up to it. Most maps and some diagrams fall into this category, but, when the object of the program is to exploit the computer's ability to process information rapidly and to represent it as a graph or a bar chart, you have to accept the computer's limitations. Apart from the question of whether the computer itself is up to the job, it is important to remember your objectives and what the program is trying to do. You will remember when we looked at 'Micro Map' (Ladybird-Longman, 1984) we noted that the authors had deliberately set out to force children to develop their mapwork skills by using and reading real maps, and with 'Rally' (Ladybird-Longman, 1984), they had deliberately set out to force children to develop speed and accuracy in performing pencil and paper tasks. If you think that the program could be enhanced by the inclusion of some pictures, diagrams or worksheets there is no reason why you should not think of the program merely as a starting point, and put them together in a study pack of your own.

Sound

      f. If sound effects are included, do they constitute an essential and integral part of the program?

Sound effects can be very useful in helping to create realism and atmosphere. A flight simulator like 'Aviator' (Acornsoft, 1983) would not be the same without the sound of the engine to give some clue as to the appropriate throttle setting. Some programs, however, include music or toots and bleeps which are totally outside the user's control, and seem to be there for no apparent reason. Probably worst of all is the program which makes a bad attempt at playing the 'Hallelujah Chorus' every time it is used. Try to think what the effect would be of using a program with sound effects in your classroom while other activities are in progress. Do you have a separate area where the computer can be used without disturbing anyone else?

      g. Does the program provide a simple means whereby the volume can be controlled or the sound can be turned off completely?

The best programs will provide these options as a matter of course, in fact some will even allow you to make adjustments throughout the program run. If things are really desperate, there are other ways of turning the sound off, but they really should not be necessary. Some computers have a command which can be typed in before the program is run, a command which should have been included as an option in the program. For example on the BBC/Acorn computer *FX 210,1 turns the sound off, and *FX 210,0 turns it back on again. Perhaps the most drastic measure, and the most permanent, is to disconnect the small loudspeaker inside the computer itself, but it really is not a good thing to 'tinker with the works' like this.

3. FRIENDLINESS AND FLEXIBILITY

'User friendliness' is a term which arises very commonly in computing circles these days. Rather than being concerned with friendliness in an anthropomorphic sense, it relates to the ease and convenience with which any program can be used, whatever its purpose. A useful, and sometimes amusing, perspective is applied to 'user friendliness' by Elithorn (1982), who draws upon his extensive experience in the use of computers for assessment testing in experimental psychology to describe what he calls 'truly ergonomic' programs. He outlines a number of 'rules', which, he considers, essential starting with one which already has been 'well learnt in educational circles'. This is that programs must be 'tailored' in such a way that they suit the needs of the user. In fact the very process of software selection, in which we are engaged, is simply a way of deciding whether a particular program is sufficiently suitable for the needs of the pupils we have in mind. Elithorn goes further, as I have done, to suggest that this tailoring process 'should be applied to the instructions as well as to the task itself'. 'Help' options are important here too. Elithorn agrees that you should always ask yourself whether the program would be easier to use 'if it had a help option available during run time'. Blank screens and obscure messages should be avoided. He writes:

> The basic principle is clear: any break in transmission should be as short as possible, or long enough to be a planned rest period or a coffee break. In starting up, for example, it is quite practicable to load a small program which will present either the instructions, or for the second time user, a summary of the key issues while the main body of the program is loading. (p.12-13)

This last point certainly echoes my own comments earlier on in this chapter. A good example of an unacceptable blank screen is in 'Quest' (AUCBE, 1983), an excellent data-base program, but when undergoing a search of a large data file, the screen can remain completely blank for several minutes during which time the user might be led to think that the program had stopped working altogether. A 'truly ergonomic' program has consistency as a key component. This means that, 'Command key press responses which cause a major state change, as for example quitting the program, should not be used elsewhere in the program for routine commands'. (p.13). This whole problem of creating and handling errors is a major bugbear in educational computing. Many programs written by amateur programmers do not take this seriously enough. It must be accepted, as a matter of course, that users will make mistakes. Elithorn's final point is that these mistakes should not prove fatal. We will take this point up further when we look at the problems of program robustness later on in this chapter.

Here are some questions you might want to ask yourself about the program:

a. Does the program provide helpful messages to correct errors?

Sometimes the only indication that you get is a cryptic message from the machine's operating system which is far from helpful. You can look up the meaning in the user manual, but even then you can't always be sure of what to do about it when you have. Good programs will tell you where you have gone wrong in plain English, and then allow you to have another go without spoiling what you have already achieved.

b. Is sufficient help provided so that pupils can understand the program without your constant intervention?

One great asset of a computer in the classroom is that it can free the teacher to concentrate on someone else in the knowledge that those using the computer are gainfully occupied. However, if it is constantly necessary to sort out queries because the program is unclear, the object is defeated. It is not just a question of poor instructions or unclear messages, it is also important to consider the level and complexity of language used, and whether it is suitable for those whom you want to use it.

c. Is the program sufficiently versatile so that the user can control what it does?

This varies, of course, as one moves from tutorials to content-free tools, but some element of choice in terms of pace and level of difficulty is desirable in most programs.

d. Is the program sufficiently flexible to be applicable in a variety of teaching/learning situations?

This raises the question of value for money. Obviously some programs are designed to do a very specific job, and if you want that job done by your computer, you must accept the cost. However, as a general rule, programs which offer several levels of difficulty, or a variety of applications to different sets of data or problems can possibly be used on more occasions and by more teachers in the school than those which have more specific and narrow applications.

4. ACHIEVEMENT OF STATED AIMS

a. Without actually using the program, and keeping your own pupils in mind, to what extent do you think the program would achieve its/your aims and objectives?

Of course at this stage there is no way of knowing for certain whether the program will ever achieve its stated aims in the classroom because you will not have had a chance to try it. For this reason this is probably the most difficult section to deal with satisfactorily. Firstly, you will need to examine the program documentation carefully to ascertain what the author says are the program's aims. You will then need to consider your own aims and objectives, and decide whether these coincide with those of the author. If they do then you need to use your own professional judgement, keeping in mind the group of children who will use the program, to decide whether it has a chance of achieving those aims and objectives. You will also need to draw upon your past experience of using computer programs in the classroom, particularly with the group of children in question. If you haven't tried any programs with this group, or this is your own first time, the decision will be rather more difficult to make. If your own aims and objectives differ from those of the program author, you will need to decide whether you could possibly use it to suit your requirements without too much difficulty. In which case you need to decide whether the program has a chance of achieving your aims and not those of the author. Once again, there will always be a degree of uncertainty, but at least you should be able to get as far as deciding whether the program is worth a trial, and as you gain experience of using programs in the classroom, the task will become easier.

If you can get hold of any case-studies written by teachers who have already used the program in the classroom, this will be a great help. There are now a number of these, called 'MEP Classroom Reports', published jointly by MEP and the Council for Educational Technology (1984 onwards).

5. ROBUSTNESS

The essence of robustness in any computer program is the degree to which it can cope with three groups of problems;

   (i) Input errors

   (ii) Unusual or unexpected inputs

   (iii) Accidental use of other keys on the keyboard.

What we are looking for then, in a good program, is the ability to deal with any of these problems without interrupting the smooth running of the program. If you are really going to test this thoroughly, you need to try every occasion when pressing a key might cause an interruption, throughout the program run. Just because the program can handle it in one place doesn't necessarily mean that it is equipped to do so everywhere.

   a. Is it easy for the user to correct typing errors?

This has already arisen when we looked at user friendliness, but it is worth looking at again. One of the major problems here is caused when the RETURN key (it may be the ENTER key on your computer), is pressed following the entry of text or data. It is usually possible to correct errors before pressing RETURN, provided that you notice them in time, but if you don't, you may have to start the program all over again. A good program will allow you to make changes to the input, through a menu option, or a command, wherever that input could have serious and far reaching effects on the result. Some programs require inputs which do not need the RETURN key to be pressed at all. These are entries of one character only, and are often used in response to a series of options in a menu, or as a simple yes/no answer to a question. Once the key is pressed there is no turning back unless the response is then 'Are you sure Y/N?' You might expect a well planned program to be consistent in its use of input methods.

b. Are possible errors trapped? When numerical input is required, what happens if you type in a word? What happens if you type in a number when a word is required?

In either case, if the program comes to an abrupt halt it means that error trapping has not been properly considered by the programmer. If you decide to continue with a program like this you are likely to find that children will be constantly asking for your help, and much time could be wasted.

c. When textual input is required, what is the longest sentence you can input? Does 'the program crash if you enter a longer one?

The most characters that many computers will allow in an input is 255, including spaces, after which the program will crash. Some will be less, but the program should handle this so that it is impossible to enter too many. This is often done by printing a simple message like 'That sentence is too long, try another'. or something like that. Of course these comments do not apply to word processors and text editors as they are specially written to handle large blocks of text.

d. Can you get all the way through the program without entering anything, just pressing the RETURN key each time a word, number or sentence is required?

A good program will always contain routines which check inputs to make sure that they are within the expected range or are of the expected kind. If the input does not fit the question, the user should be told why it was unsuitable, and invited to try again.

e. When numerical input is required, what happens if you type in very large or very small numbers?

f. Can the program cope with an input of zero or a negative number?

If the program has to perform some calculations, numbers outside its expected range can cause unusual results or cause the program to crash altogether. Very large or very small numbers can create results which are beyond the scope of the model, division by zero will cause the program to crash unless the input is properly checked by a special routine before any calculations are performed.

g. Are all non-essential keys automatically turned off by the program itself? Try pressing some wrong keys, e.g. ESCAPE, BREAK, SHIFT/BREAK, the CONTROL key in conjunction with any others.

While the program is running the only keys which should have any effect are those essential to the activity. If any other key is pressed by mistake, nothing should happen. With most computers it is a simple matter to cater for this when the program is being written. The key which probably causes the most problems is the BREAK key, especially if it is situated in a prominent position, or is near to other keys which might be regularly used as the program is running. Some programs overcome this problem by using it to return the user to the main menu, at any time, without causing a break.

SPECIFIC SELECTION CRITERIA

Having looked at those selection criteria which might apply generally to nearly all programs, we need to consider those which may be especially important to particular kinds of programs.

(i) Tutorial and drill and practice programs

Although there are some significant differences between these two kinds of program, they have several things in common which are concerned with content, accuracy, input style, feedback, pupil records, and other non computer-based work.

a. Is the content fully described?

b. Is the content of the program appropriate to the designer's stated aims and objectives?

c. Is the content and presentation appropriate to your class and the use you have in mind?

d. Is the micro appropriate for teaching this topic?

These first four are all closely related. In fact they could probably be combined into one, but I have separated them for the sake of clarity. Obviously it makes the selection task easier if you can read about the program content before you try it. But also, in school, it is useful to be able to refer to the documentation now and again to remind yourself of the content. The question of appropriate content has arisen elsewhere, but this time you need to decide whether, in your opinion, the content matches the designer's and your own aims and objectives sufficiently to be worth using. However, you might feel that there are better ways of covering the same ground, and will consequently reject the program.

    e. Is the content/information accurate?

    f. Is the content/information accurate enough for the use you have in mind?

The question of accuracy is a very important one, and can arise in two ways. Firstly, if the program is simply imparting information like most tutorials do, you have to be sure that that information is correct. Secondly, if the program requires some numerical input from the user in order to perform a calculation, you need to be sure that the range of acceptable inputs is controlled by the program so that the outcome is an acceptable fit to observations made in the real world. Of course, sometimes certain approximations or simplifications are acceptable in order that an idea is easier to grasp. This is not uncommon in science and economics for example. You only need to be sure that the information is accurate enough for your purposes, given that you have a particular group of pupils in mind.

    g. Does the input format suit your purposes? Are there options from which you can choose?

Remember the example of drill and practice programs involving multiplication. Would you prefer the children to be able to enter their answers as they work them out, or do you want them to perform paper and pencil tasks? A good program will give you the option, or at least justify the choice of input format in the documentation.

    h. Does the program provide immediate and appropriate feedback to the user?

Behaviourist theories of learning stress the importance of regular and positive feedback to the learner. This means that all desirable behaviour or correct responses need to be rewarded. However, undesirable behaviour or incorrect responses are best ignored in the sense that an absence of positive feedback is feedback enough. Some programs, in trying to supply negative feedback to discourage incorrect responses, actually defeat their own objective since the so-called negative feedback is often more entertaining than the positive variety.

The result is that the undesirable responses are encouraged.

   i. Does the program keep a score or a record of the
      learner's progress?

This is useful from a diagnostic point of view, although a
scoring or points system is probably more useful as a
motivating factor. Learners can try to improve their own
personal scores, or they can compete against one another. It is
useful sometimes, however, to be able to turn off the scoring
facility, especially if you think that it could cause too much
anxiety in a particular child. A more detailed record of the
learner's progress is very useful for the teacher as a
diagnostic aid, and can be the subject of discussion between
the teacher and the learner at a later stage. Once again,
however, it ought to be available as an option since it can
sometimes be seen as 'spying' and ought not to be used without
the pupil's knowledge.

   j. Does the program suggest pencil and paper tasks, or
      other work that might be carried out away from the
      computer?

Work cards, references for private study, art and craft, drama
and so on are all activities which can be used to follow up a
tutorial or a drill and practice program. Some of the best
program packs contain a whole range of ideas like this which
will help you to integrate the program fully into the normal
range of classroom activities.

For Tutorial programs in particular

   k. Is the content broken down into appropriately small and
      logical stages?

   l. Does the program allow the user to revise previous
      pages or follow remedial loops?

   m. Will the program take free-format answers in an
      acceptable number of forms?

These three points are more specific to the smooth running and
convenience of use of tutorial programs. Each frame needs to be
simple enough for the user to be almost guaranteed success, and
the frames must be presented in a logical sequence. Whenever a
difficulty arises it should be possible to revise or to be
automatically sent round a remedial loop until the point has
been clarified and understood. When input is required from the
learner, it is important that the program is sufficiently
versatile to accept answers in a variety of forms, even to the
extent of catering for the more common spelling mistakes if

accurate spelling is not the major purpose of the activity.

For drill and practice programs in particular

    n. Does the program provide a variety of levels of difficulty?

    o. Are the examples or exercises randomly generated?

Obviously the more levels of difficulty available in a program, the more use you will have for it. Also, any one pupil will be spared the boredom of working through the same examples over and over again. This is further aided if the examples themselves are randomly generated so that they never follow a set sequence. If all of the examples are contained in the program as Data, they very soon become exhausted and the pupils come to learn which one is coming next. You should expect to find details of how the examples are generated, somewhere in the program documentation.

(ii) Arcade-type games

    a. Are the instructions clear and always available?

Remember that it is a good thing to be able to refer to the instructions while the program is running.

    b. Does the program provide a sufficient range of levels of difficulty and speed?

    c. Is the content of the program available for inspection and/or change?

    d. Is the content accurate?

Especially in the case of matching, sequencing and reading exercises, it is useful to be able to preview the content in the form of a word or sound list. Some programs will allow you to make changes or additions to this list, which of course makes them more versatile. If they do not, then you must decide whether the list is sufficiently comprehensive for your purposes.

    e. Does the program provide appropriate feedback to the player?

    f. Does the program keep a score or a record of the player's progress?

The same comments apply here as they did when we looked at

tutorial and drill and practice programs.

g. Is the visual display likely to be attractive, exciting
and absorbing?

Remember that arcade-type games are often used to add interest
and excitement to an otherwise dull activity. Children become
so absorbed in playing the game that they forget that, in order
to progress, they are actually having to learn and practice new
skills.

(iii) Simulation games

a. Is it appropriate to use the computer for this topic?

b. Is the content of the program appropriate to your aims
and to the group you have in mind?

c. Are commands and instructions available throughout the
program run?

These three have all arisen before, leading on to the next
question which is particularly relevant to adventure type
simulations,

d. Does the program (or the documentation) give sufficient
and appropriate clues if the user gets stuck?

e. Is the nature of the model made explicit?

You will find this particularly helpful when you are trying to
select an appropriate simulation game for your class. It should
help you finally to make decisions about how appropriate the
program is.

f. Is there provision to change data if appropriate?
This does not necessarily apply to all simulations, but in
cases like 'Micro Map'(Ladybird-Longman, 1985) it is a great
asset.

g. Can a game be 'saved' and resumed later?

Sometimes complicated simulation games take longer to complete
that you have time available. It is very frustrating if every
time, you must start again from the beginning. If the current
game can be saved on tape or disc, next time the players can
just start where they left off.

h. Does the program give any suggestions as to how it
might relate to events in the real world?

Suggestions for follow-up work which include a wide range of other activities may be very helpful in getting the pupils to relate their work with the computer to their everyday experiences.

(iv) Laboratory simulations

a. Is the nature of the mathematical model made specific?

b. Is the range and degree of accuracy of the model discussed in the documentation?

In laboratory simulations the mathematical model is of particular importance since very often the purpose of such a simulation is for the user to come to understand more fully the theoretical basis of the model itself. For this reason, you must be sure that it does not over-simplify the problem or make it so complicated as to defeat its own, or your, objectives.

c. Is there provision for changing the data?

The best programs will allow you to do this by selecting the appropriate option, but alas, some might expect you to follow instructions and 'tinker with the code'.

d. Could this topic be covered more effectively with real practical work?

Remember that laboratory simulations can only effectively replace first-hand experience if that experience would prove to be too expensive, too dangerous or too time-consuming.

(v) Content-free tools

The essence of all good content-free tools, that is data-bases, teletext emulators, word processors and programming languages is that they are relatively 'transparent'. That is, they are convenient to use without getting in the way. Of all these, it is probably the data-bases which create the most initial confusion so I will make some particular comments about these,

Data-bases

When creating files,

a. Are the instructions clear and easy to follow?

b. What is the maximum number of records and fields?

    c. What is the maximum field size?

    d. Is there an option to edit and delete records?

    e. Can the number of records be increased after the file
       has been created?

If you want to create fairly large data files you will need to
select a data-base which stores its files on disc rather than
in its own memory. This means that you can handle a large
number of records relatively quickly. Make sure that the
maximum number of fields is not too small, some of the best
data-bases for school use allow up to at least twenty. If you
have some idea of the kind of data you might collect you will
have an idea of how large each field will need to be. Remember
that if you have many large fields in a data file, you will
have less room available for individual records. Finally, it is
always useful to be able to add more records at a later date,
so make sure that the program allows this as well as an option
to edit, add and delete records.

When interrogating files,

    f. Are the instructions for formulating a query clear and
       unambiguous?

    g. Is there a 'help' option to explain the commands and to
       describe the fields?

    h. Does the search option allow you to formulate both
       simple and complex queries?

    i. What is the longest query acceptable?

When you first come to use a data-base you will need all the
help you can get. It is therefore important that the
instructions and 'help' routines are as explicit as possible.
It is always useful to be able to perform a search for several
attributes at the same time, so make sure that the program you
choose allows for this unless you are going to be working with
very young children, where perhaps one or maybe two will be
enough. If you look back to the section on data-bases in
chapter three (p.50), you will find a list of the kinds of
search facilities to look out for.

USING OTHER PEOPLE'S ASSESSMENTS

It is hoped that the discussion of the selection criteria in
the previous sections will, in conjunction with your own

experience of using a computer in the classroom, help you review and select suitable software. I have tried to cover as many of the points that arise in most check-lists, but of course there is always the chance that you might find others which you would prefer to add or even use instead. Clearly, the comments and guidelines which I have offered represent my own feelings about sofware selection in the light of my own experience and research, and there are bound to be those who would wish to take me to task on some of them. However, if you adopt them as general, though not hard and fast, guidelines, you will not go far wrong.

There will be times, however, when you have the opportunity to see program assessments or reviews written by other teachers who may have had the opportunity to use the program in the classroom. Here are a number of fundamental questions which you could ask yourself about them to help you assess their validity, and therefore their usefulness when deciding whether the program would suit your needs.

1. How reliable is the information? To what extent does it represent the behaviour of the audience of the age and ability range for which it was intended? Does it give any indication of the problems encountered by poor performers?

2. How accurate is the information? As far as you can tell, has the full range of effects (positive and negative), been accurately identified and reported? To what extent have the effects claimed actually been measured? How well does the evaluator know the program?

3. How discriminating is the information? To what extent does it reflect differences in responses among the target audience? Does it indicate the conditions which resulted in different responses?

4. How useful is the information? Has it told you anything you wouldn't already have known? Does it suggest practical changes that could be made, or problems to be avoided when using the program?

5. To what extent does it take the context into account? How did the program relate to other media or fit into the curriculum? How was the program used by the teacher and/or the learners?

(Adapted from Bates (1981), pp.230-31)

Chapter Five

USING EDUCATIONAL SOFTWARE

So far we have concentrated our attention on the selection of
software which we, as teachers, think might serve as useful
teaching and learning resources in the classroom. I have
emphasised that the decisions we make about the suitability of
programs must always be made in the light of the role they
might play within the overall curriculum objectives of the
school, and our lesson objectives for a particular class or
group of pupils. What may be the right choice in one school, or
with one group of children, may not be so in different
circumstances. As a consequence of this, teachers may find
themselves having to regularly make judgements about the
suitability of computer programs even though they have had some
considerable classroom experience with those programs already.
Of course this is nothing new, it is a common process in
teaching, being one of the most important skills exhibited by
teachers when matching curriculum content, resources and ideas
to what they know about the strengths, weaknesses, abilities
and interests of their pupils. As classroom experience of a
program increases, and it is tried with a wider variety of
classes, the decision process becomes more automatic, and can
be made without further reference to check-lists, reviews, or
dare I say, even the program documentation. However, as I have
pointed out earlier, software selection is one thing, but
software evaluation is quite another. Once a program has been
selected for classroom use because it appears to fulfil a set
of minimum requirements or to match an agreed set of selection
criteria, it is important to have some measure or means of
assessment of its effectiveness as a teaching and learning
resource when actually in use. If the process of critical
review and appraisal of educational software stops at the point
when the resource is purchased or acquired, then the job has
been abandoned only half completed. Computer programs are no
different to all other educational resources, which need to be
evaluated in the classroom. This does not, and need not, always
take the form of a formal evaluation under so-called

'laboratory conditions', but will nevertheless be influential in helping teachers make decisions about the suitability of resources for the future.

EVALUATION IN THE CLASSROOM

No doubt you will be thinking that the prospect of having to evaluate your computer programs in the classroom, while teaching a full timetable and trying to come to terms with the technology itself, is just asking too much. In recent years, however, there has been a growing trend for serving teachers to become more and more interested and involved in classroom-based observation or research. More and more teachers are attempting to formally evaluate the effectiveness of their teaching and the usefulness of the resources that they use. By undertaking research in their own classrooms, many teachers feel that they can take increased responsibility for their actions, creating a more energetic and dynamic environment in which teaching and learning can take place. For years educational research has been dominated by outsiders. Even the choice of problems to be investigated has been in the hands of those who are strong on research expertise but have little recent experience in the classroom. Surely, at the local level at least, it is those who work in the schools day-in day-out who are best qualified to decide which issues are the most pressing for investigation. What we are really talking about here is small-scale curriculum research and development, conducted by serving teachers in relation to the curriculum and resources of their own schools. Since the new technology of the microcomputer age has, and will continue to have, such far-reaching implications for curriculum development and change, it is important that teachers should be able to investigate its implications and effectiveness for themselves. One of the major exponents of the 'teacher as researcher' movement was Lawrence Stenhouse who, having directed the Humanities Curriculum Project, made it the major theme of one of his best known books, 'An introduction to Curriculum Research and Development' (Stenhouse, 1975). For Stenhouse, well-founded curriculum research and development;

> ...whether the work of an individual teacher, of a school, of a group working in a teacher's centre, or a group working within the co-ordinating framework of a national project, is based on the study of classrooms. It thus rests on the work of teachers.
>   It is not enough that teachers' work should be studied: they need to study it themselves. (p.143)

In describing the teacher best suited to this kind of work, Stenhouse develops the idea of 'extended professionalism' first proposed by Hoyle (1972). He attempts to define what he calls 'the outstanding characteristics of the extended professional' in the following way;

> The critical characteristics of that extended professionalism which is essential for well-founded curriculum research and development seem to me to be:
>
> The commitment to systematic questioning of one's own teaching as a basis for development;
> The commitment and the skills to study one's own teaching;
> The concern to question and to test theory in practice by the use of those skills.
>
> To these may be added as highly desirable, though perhaps not essential, a readiness to allow other teachers to observe one's work - directly or through recordings - and to discuss it with them on an open and honest basis. (p.144)

Clearly, there will be many teachers who would find it difficult to identify with this image of the extended professional. It is not that they would not like to be that way, indeed many teachers welcome the opportunity to discuss their work with colleagues, and even to observe others working or be observed themselves. The problem in many cases, however, is how to acquire what they imagine to be the necessary research skills in order to make a start. The fact is, of course, that most people are led to believe that there is something sacred about 'research' which legitimately makes it the sole domain of those who work in the ivory towers of higher education. Nothing could be further from the truth. Is it not a strange irony that some teachers spend so much time developing childrens' ability to formulate and test hypotheses, and to collect, weigh-up and assess evidence, but feel ill-equipped to apply the same skills to the evaluation of their own performance and resources? What I will try to illustrate in the rest of this chapter, are a number of simple ways in which teachers can set about evaluating the effectiveness of computer software. In so doing, we might hope to raise the process of software evaluation to a level beyond that of mere subjective impression.

WAYS OF LOOKING AT THE PROBLEM

It is true, in all walks of life, that there is always more than one way of looking at a problem. This is no less true for educational research even in its most humble form. In fact many researchers in the social sciences make good use of this fact by seeking research evidence from a number of different angles in the hope that the results will mutually, but independently, support their original hypotheses. This is a research technique commonly known as 'triangulation'. In our particular case, should we try to measure differences in performance and subject the results to statistical analysis, or would it be more useful to make informal observations which could be recorded in the form of a diary? Would it not be better to construct a check-list of desired behaviour characteristics and use that as a guide whilst observing children using the computer, or should we interview the children and ask them to complete a questionnaire after each session using a particular program? Obviously there are many ways to approach the problem of evaluating computer programs in the classroom, but in general they can be sub-divided into two broad categories based upon the nature of the data to be collected and the use to which it may be put. The first category contains all those approaches which involve measurement of some kind which may, in certain circumstances, be suitable for statistical analysis. These are called quantitative methods. Those which do not involve measurement, but require the collection of people's views or impressions, or set out to describe how a program has been used, or the behaviour of the children while using it are basically descriptive and are called qualitative methods. Of course the distinction between the two is not always quite so distinct. It is possible that some subjective views or impressions can be expressed and categorised in such a way that they can be subjected to a form of statistical analysis which may not be generalizable to the wider population, but can tell us some useful things about those children using the program. Indeed there is a very strong case for combining quantitative and qualitative evidence as a means of acquiring a broader picture of how effective a program might be.

QUANTITATIVE APPROACHES

It was not unusual in the past for quantitative investigations of educational problems to be staged in psychological laboratories rather than in real classrooms. Of course such practices have their usefulness, but at the same time they have been heavily criticised. They are so unlike real classrooms that very little can be inferred from one about the other. Nevertheless, when people started to think about investigating real problems in real classrooms, many attempted to transfer those laboratory methods into the classroom. These we might rightly call 'laboratory-type' experiments, which although conducted in an on-going classroom situation depend very much upon the comparison of the performance of experimental and control groups. If, for example, one group is taught a topic by more conventional methods, while another is taught using a specific computer program, and a third group is not taught that topic at all, a statistical comparison of test results of

all three groups both before and after the experiment might be
expected to reveal what effect the program had in comparison to
conventional teaching or no teaching at all. It is very often
assumed that if the experimental group comes out best, then the
educational superiority of the method used with that group has
been proved. For such an approach to be at all valid, however,
it is necessary to ensure that all variables other than those
under scrutiny are eliminated or controlled. The pupils used in
each group must be closely matched for such things as sex, age,
ability, previous experience with the computer, the program or
even programs of its type. How can you control for differences
in the 'quality of presentation' to the different groups when
different methods or media are being used? How do you know
that the quality of presentation of a computer program – one
that exploits the potential of the medium – is equivalent in
quality to the presentation in a book or a lecture or a
television program? In fact there is very good reason for
suggesting that;

> One of the clearer findings from experimental research is
> that learning gains tend to vary more within than between
> media. (Bates, 1981 p.221)

As you can see, not only is this very difficult to do with any
degree of certainty, but by the time it has been done, what
remains hardly matches what we might call a normal teaching and
learning environment. The result of all this is that such
controlled experiments take place in somewhat artificial
conditions. What is important to realise is that such
experiments are unlikely to be part of a normal everyday
teaching program in that they do not sufficiently represent the
situation in which the program to be evaluated would normally
be used. Even if all of these problems can be overcome, it is
not always easy or even possible to pinpoint or isolate what it
is about a particular program that makes it so effective.

Now, having read this you might well be wondering why we
should bother with quantitative methods at all. In actual
fact, it is possible for individuals or groups of teachers to
use these kinds of methods quite effectively in their own
classrooms. By virtue of the fact that they are already there,
and are an integral part of the action, alterations to the
normal class groupings or changes to the normal class routines
are far less noticeable or traumatic for the pupils than if
they had been initiated by a group of strangers who had
arrived unannounced to conduct an isolated experiment and then
gone away again. Within an individual class, matched groups
could be given time to settle down before the actual experiment
is conducted, children can be given time to get used to the
idea of small groups being taught by different methods or even
different teachers without any sudden and traumatic changes to
classroom routines. At this point it might be useful to look at

Using Educational Software

an example of a simple experiment conducted by a teacher in her
own classroom, with a little help from some interested
colleagues.

A STUDY OF PROGRAM EFFECTIVENESS

Denise Randell set about testing the effectiveness of a drill
and practice program with three fourth year mixed ability
classes in Great Glen primary school, Leicestershire, where she
was teaching. The program she chose was 'Rally - A'
(Ladybird-Longman 1984), which simulates a car rally in which
the children have to drive the car from town to town using the
least amount of fuel in the shortest time possible. In order to
collect enough fuel to complete the journey it is necessary to
answer some problems in the form of sums. These can be set at a
variety of levels of difficulty using any of the four rules.
This is how she describes what she did;

> The main aim of the study was to test the hypothesis that
> using a drill and practice computer program as part of a
> mathematics teaching scheme would affect a child's
> performance with respect to accuracy and speed. At the
> same time I tried to investigate whether the degree of the
> childrens' "computer awareness", the degree of teacher
> involvement and the type of teacher talk affected the
> overall results.
> It was decided to consider the accuracy variable as the
> number of sums correct divided by the number of sums
> attempted and to express this as a percentage.... The
> variable depicting speed would show the number of sums
> attempted in the given time.
> As the group of children to which the tests were to be
> given are of mixed ability and taught by three teachers,
> it was necessary to include sums which were appropriate
> for all the levels of ability. The number program to be
> used was designed for practising computational skills and
> could be operated at one of three levels. In practice it
> was decided to concentrate on 'Rally - A'
> (Ladybird - Longman, 1984), because this would mean that
> all the children could use the program, regardless of
> their level of ability. Therefore the mathematics test
> sheets to be attempted before and after using the program
> had to be devised accordingly. As the children were to be
> tested twice, this necessitated two tests to be devised
> which were of the same level of difficulty and made up of
> a similar selection of sums in the correct proportions.
> Therefore it was thought advisable to refer to a published
> selection of graded sums, (K.A.Hesse, 'The Four Rules of
> Number') in the hope of overcoming any bias when compiling

the test sheets.

The written instructions were kept to a minimum of name and date, and the children were told to record the time at the beginning of the test and the time at which they finnished, or were told to stop by the teacher.

Initially forty-five children were included in the sample, but due to absence only forty children took part in all the test stages. As the children were divided into three unequal groups for the teaching of maths, it was decided to rank them on the basis of their NFER. DEl standardised scores before systematically selecting the four groups for the study in order to try to avoid any bias in the selection procedure.

The four groups were called A,B,C and D, each consisting of children of mixed ability to try to make sure that the control and experimental groups were properly matched. Groups A and B were to have differing degrees of computer experience, but have the same teacher involvement and teacher talk. Groups C and D were to have identical computer experience, with different teacher involvement. A prepared script was used by the teacher when she was working with group D. It did not include any personal comments or words of encouragement from the teacher who tried to adopt a neutral approach. On the other hand, when working with group C, the teacher returned to her individual teaching style which many of the children were familiar with.

Maths Test Sheet 1, (the pre - test) was done by all children at the same time. Each group then started its own schedule. The children had individual record books in which they noted any previous experience of 'playing' with a similar computer or a type of computer game. After their 'hands - on' time, they recorded their results and their thoughts about their experience.

Group A's schedule began with a general introduction, which explained the relevant parts of the system. Then they worked with the BBC 'Keyboard' program on the Welcome tape for fifteen minutes. This was done because it was felt that familiarity with the keyboard, reading, understanding and following instructions from the screen, and generally becoming more confident about using the computer before using the program may influence their attitude, approach and level of attainment.

Group B did not have any keyboard experience and started using the program immediately, each child having fifteen minutes hands - on experience.

Group C experienced the general introduction, the keyboard familiarity exercise and the 'Rally' program. Group D had the general introduction, the keyboard familiarity exercise and the 'Rally' program, but the teacher used the script when speaking to them.

The day after experiencing the 'Rally' program each child performed Maths Test sheet 2, (the post - test) consisting of sixty sums to be completed in fifteen minutes.

The results were recorded for each group and a 't' - test was used for the statistical analysis. I was looking for any statistically significant difference between the scores on the pre and the post tests for each of the groups. The 't' - test operates by testing the 'null hypothesis' that there would be no statistically significant change in the speed or accuracy of performance for any of the four groups of children. An examination of the results showed that there did not appear to be a statistically significant improvement in performance of any of the groups taking part in the study where accuracy is concerned. However, there was a highly significant improvement in performance when speed was considered. It was also interesting to note that the improvement in speed was greater for the upper third of the ability range. This was also true for the accuracy results although they were not, in themselves, statistically significant. However, one must bear in mind that the children only had fifteen minutes experience with 'Rally', and perhaps this was insufficient time for 'accuracy' to be improved.....

The aim of this experiment was to test the hypothesis that using a drill and practice computer program as a part of a maths scheme will affect the childrens' performance with respect to speed and accuracy. The results have shown that the childrens' performance did improve with respect to speed after experiencing such a program for only fifteen minutes. However, there did not appear to be a statistically significant difference for accuracy in such a short period of time.

In retrospect I feel that 'Rally' actually achieves what it was designed to achieve. At the same time motivating, giving confidence to and making everyday drill and practice routine part of an exercise that all children can experience.

Clearly this study attempts to look at more than just the effect of the program on the speed and accuracy of the childrens' computation skills, but I have only included the conclusions which relate to the main hypothesis since they are sufficient to illustrate how the study was conducted. In normal circumstances, teaching style, teacher involvement and computer familiarity would all be variables which need to be controlled as far as possible. In other words care must be taken to ensure that their effect is the same for all groups. In fact, this experiment would have been even more revealing if one group (the 'control' group), had received identical treatment to the others, but with no experience of the 'Rally' program itself. If this had happened, it would have been clearer whether it was the program which made the difference to the children's speed scores, or whether it was something else quite different. It is an important condition of quantitative studies of this kind that the control group receives exactly the same treatment as the others except for the one variable which is being tested. If this condition can be met, any differences in performance can be more reasonably attributed to changes in that variable rather than any other.

The other improvement which could be made, of course, is to allow for much longer periods of time spent actually using the program. This could be done over a period of several days or even weeks. If this were done there would be a better chance of seeing some change in the accuracy scores as well as some levelling off of the speed scores between the least and the most able children. Denise Randell was well aware of these problems at the time, but due to the pressure of other school commitments at that time of year, she had to compromise somewhat. For example she notes that there is always a possibility of improvement in performance simply as a result of newly introduced change, and was fully prepared for a certain amount of criticism on the grounds that fifteen minutes experience was too little.

A SIMPLE PRE-TEST, POST-TEST DESIGN

If you are not too happy about using statistical tests like correlation coefficients, 't' tests and so on, it is possible to get some idea of how effective a computer program is by using simple percentages. You would not be in a position to make any hard and fast claims about the validity of your results, but perhaps, within the confines of your own classroom, it would at least provide more systematic evidence than previously available to you. This was the approach adopted by Ward, et al (1985), when they attempted an evaluation of software developed to enable hearing-impaired children to explore and experience the use and effects of language. Although part of this experiment was conducted by outside researchers, it was done with the full participation of the teachers concerned, and being very much a 'classroom study', could just as easily have been under the teachers' complete control. The software was designed to allow interactive graphics to be discussed and controlled by means of what they called a 'simple "natural" language interface' so that the user could hold a written conversation with the computer. Using one of several vocabularies ranging from ten phrases to over forty, the system allows sentences to be built up word by word or phrase by phrase. This will allow for the construction of approximately forty to ten thousand 'acceptable' sentences, and the computer can also provide feedback about 'unacceptable' sentences containing syntax or other errors. What they were interested to assess was whether making written language interactive, would allow prelingually deaf children to use, in the written medium, language learning strategies similar to those normally used by hearing children in the spoken medium. As in the previous example, they used a simple pre-test, post-test design, but expressed the results as straightforward percentages of errors or correct responses.

The classroom study was conducted with six hearing-impaired teenagers whose mean chronological age was 14 years 2 months, and whose mean reading age was 7 years 1 month. They worked for one hour a week for twelve weeks on a total of six programs. For the most part they worked individually, except for the support of a teacher or researcher.

The design of appropriate pre- and post-tests is a crucial part of this kind of evaluation. In this case, a specially designed game was played between subject and researcher for about twenty minutes on each occasion. The subjects and researchers communicated by pointing to words on a vocabulary card. This is how it is described by the authors;

> As the software covers a restricted linguistic domain, its use is unlikely to lead to gains measurable by global tests of reading ability. A two-person non-computer-based game was therefore devised to serve as a pre-test and post-test of subjects' ability to construct sentences and to use language purposefully. The game involved subject and experimenter in a dialogue concerned with the hiding and finding of familiar real-life objects. Each had a set of six small drawers arranged in two rows of three, and a set of twelve objects for placing in the drawers. The objects were string, a screwdriver, a large and a small rubber, a large and a small battery, and three crayons and three sweets coloured red, yellow and blue. Both middle bottom drawers were coloured yellow to be used as a reference. A vocabulary card was used as a communication aid, and this displayed the following words: the, blue, red, yellow, large, small, battery, crayon, drawer, rubber, screwdriver, string, sweet, put, move, is, in, left, of, over, right, to, under, what, where, yes, no. (p68)

The game itself was arranged in four parts or conditions, the first of which was intended to familiarise the subject with how the game was to be played:

> In all conditions the two sets of drawers were positioned

so that the subject and experimenter could see only their own set. In condition 1 the experimenter hid six items, one in each drawer, and then constructed six imperative 'put' sentences so that the subject could replicate the pattern of hidden items. The main purpose of this condition was to introduce subjects to the idea of the game, and no data was collected. Condition 2 was similar to condition 1 except that the roles of the hider and the replicator were reversed. In condition 3 it was again the subject who did the hiding, but this time the experimenter obtained information about the items by asking the subject questions. Condition 4 was similar to condition 3 but with the roles of hider and questioner reversed. In conditions 1 and 4 the objects hidden by the experimenter, and their positions, were constant across subjects and from pre-test to post-test. Also constant were the sentences used by the experimenter in condition 1, and the positional and referential order of the questions asked by the experimenter in condition 3. (pp.68-69)

As you can see, a great deal of trouble was taken to devise tests which would be sufficiently specific to the tasks involved in the computer programs, as well as sufficiently sensitive to detect any appreciable changes in the subjects' performance after using it. Unlike the previous example, a more realistic time was allowed for the subjects to use and possibly learn from the programs, but unfortunately no control group was included. To have included such a control group would have been quite easy since, in this case, it only required a similar group of pupils to undertake the pre- and the post-test without having any contact with the computer programs in between. Even if to do this had raised questions about the ethics of using children as experimental subjects, giving some preferential treatment at the expense of others, it could be ensured that all pupils had a chance to use the programs, even if some did so after the experiment had been completed.

In order to compare the relative incidence of syntax errors in the pre-test and post-test, each subject's best six sentences per condition were taken. In the pre-test, syntax errors occured in 45% of cases whereas in the post-test their incidence was reduced to 25%;

This suggests possible improvements in subjects' abilities to construct syntactically acceptable sentences within the domain of language covered by the software. The reduction in the number of qualitatively different types of error from 27 to 16 is another indicator of this trend. (p.70)

It is worth noting here that the authors were aware that the scale and scope of their investigation only allowed them to draw conclusions within the 'domain of the language covered by the software'. In addition you should be aware that with such a small group of subjects, and collecting such a small amount of data, the results can only be used as a very rough guide as to whether the software is being effective or not. Certainly, for example, it would not be possible to draw any hard and fast conclusions about the effectiveness of the software with a wider population. If the authors had included a control group as I have suggested, it would have been possible to attribute the gains in performance to the programs with a great deal more certainty. As it stands, we will never be completely sure whether it was the software that did the trick, or whether it was really due to something quite different.

A FEW SIMPLE RULES

So, having looked at these two examples of simple pre-test, post-test designs, we could draw up a set of simple rules or guidelines for those who wish to try them out in their own classrooms:

If you feel that using a controlled experiment is the best way to evaluate the effectiveness of a computer program with your pupils in your own classroom, then;

1. Match your experimental groups carefully, and in such a way that it creates the minimum of disturbance to the day-to-day classroom routine. It may be of importance to you to find out about the effectiveness of the program, but it should not be done at your pupils' expense.

2. Always use a control group.

3. Make sure that the control group receives <u>exactly</u> the same treatment as the rest <u>except</u> for the one variable you are testing.

4. Be sure to allow sufficient time for effects to emerge, if they are going to emerge at all.

5. Be careful not to draw too many conclusions from research with small groups and small amounts of data. Remember that with small samples, the differences in performance between pre-test and post-test must be very large in order to be statistically significant.

USING AN EVALUATION CHECKLIST

The controlled experiment approach may be quite suitable for the evaluation of computer programs of a tutorial or drill and practice kind, especially those leading to tangible differences in performance which can be measured in some way. However, this is not always so, or you may feel that it is a very different sort of feedback that you require. Some teachers and researchers prefer to use checklists which are rather like those used for software selection, but with the checklist items slanted more towards the users feelings about, or reactions towards the program during or after its use. While the user's responses are of a more qualitative kind, the design of the checklist can allow for a certain amount of quantitative treatment of the responses.

A PUPILS' CHECKLIST

A particularly useful example of this approach may be found amongst the MEP 'Classroom Reports' (Blunt, 1984), which sets out to evaluate a content-free tool called 'Tray' in a modern languages classroom at The Grange School, Warmley, in Avon. The program is designed so that the teacher can choose a piece of text which has linguistic qualities which are integral to the recent work of the class. The user being confronted with the punctuation of the text only, has the option of buying letters which are then printed in wherever they appear in the text, or of predicting the exact place where a letter will appear. If the user buys letters, points are lost, whereas if letter positions are successfully predicted, points are gained. As Blunt so rightly points out;

> There are other commands and refinements, but simply at this level the potential for the good or bad use of the software is evident. A successful strategy rests on the ability to predict letter, sound, word or phrase patterns, whereas just guessing turns it into an unrewarding game. (p.10)

Following the use of the program by twenty-nine fourth year 'O' level students, the chosen text being in French, the teachers involved commented that both levels of motivation and rate of acquisition of the target language had been improved. However, these comments were not entirely subjective in nature, since the teachers made their judgements with particular reference to the students' workbooks and their answers to questions.

More importantly from our point of view, the teachers at The Grange School devised for themselves an evaluation checklist which was to be completed by the students after using the program. Following that, it was possible to tabulate the results in such a way that a clearer view could be obtained of the students' overall reactions to the program.

The checklist was divided into three main sections, concentrating on work with the computer, work with the booklet, and general comments on the whole work.

1. Work with the computer.

In this first section students were invited to answer questions about;

a. their previous experience of computers,

b. the quality and quantity of the instructions given at the beginning of the lesson, and how much they referred to the instruction card while using the program,

c. the difficulty of the chosen text,

d. their feelings about working on the program in a group,

e. their feelings about how often, if at all, they would like to have sessions with the computer in the future.

2. Work with the booklet.

In this second section students were invited to comment on;

a. whether they found the work in the booklet either boring, useful, alright, or enjoyable,

b. and to suggest which parts of the work were most or least enjoyable, boring or useful.

3. General comments on the whole work.

In the third and final section students were invited to comment on;

a. how much they felt they had learnt in comparison with other, more conventional lessons,

b. the extent to which the booklet was useful to further the work,

c. those things that they felt they had actually learnt,

d. whether they could think of any other comments not included in the checklist,

e. whether they had felt that the exercise was more like work or play to them.

Since 'Tray' is a content-free tool, its use will always depend upon the type, quality and suitability of the text chosen by the teacher. This means that any evaluation using the checklist will be very specific to the program and chosen text, but never the program on its own. This is something which is common to the evaluation of all content-free software since without content the software could not be evaluated at all. This being so, the question must always arise as to the suitability of the content for treatment using that particular tool, and hence the need to ask questions about the choice of text and the quality of the content of the booklet.

A TEACHERS' CHECKLIST

In the previous example the checklist was designed to elicit the feelings and reactions of those who actually used the program, the pupils. It is, of course, possible to use a similar instrument which you or your own colleagues fill in after using the program with a class or groups of children. Clearly the questions which are appropriate for this task will be different from those you might ask the children themselves, and will be more concerned with educational aims and objectives. However, unlike the checklists used for software selection, the rating criteria ought to provide ample opportunity for users to make less speculative judgements based upon their real experience using the program with children in a normal classroom setting. One such instrument has been suggested by Blake (1984), which invites the user to rate the program on a five-point scale for each of thirty eight rating criteria, according to whether each is near perfect, above average, average, below average, or unacceptable. The only stipulation made about use of the program is that the teacher should have at least two hours experience of it with a class or classes. I include this particular piece of work as an example simply because it appears on a reading list published by MEP, therefore presumably recomended by them, but is unobtainable from the source listed. Like so many other so-called rating scales the criteria themselves come with little explanation, and so are left very much to the interpretation of individual users. However, if an individual teacher or a small group within one school were to adopt it as a model for designing their own rating scale, some form of working consensus could easily be achieved. Following the program's use with several groups of children in the school the teachers' rating summaries could be kept with the program or filed in a convenient place in the staffroom library for future reference. Here are the 38 rating criteria. Remember that they do not have to be adopted as they stand, in fact they may require extensive revision before they suit the needs and interests of most teachers working in particular classroom environments, but I include them here to give you a better idea of how you might go about agreeing upon a set of your own,

1. Effectiveness of objective 1.

2. Effectiveness of objective 2.

3. Effectiveness of objective 3.

4. Overall educational value.

5. Overall ease of use.

6. Overall impact.

7. Initial impact.

8. Ability to maintain attention.

9. Density of information screen.

10. Screen layout.

11. Rate of appearance of information on screen.

12. Grammar, punctuation, spelling.

13. Clarity of messages.

14. Effectiveness of use of colour.

15. Effectiveness of use of sound.

16. Effectiveness of use of graphs/charts.

17. Effectiveness of use of graphics.

18. Effectiveness of use of animations.

19. Adequacy of self-pacing.

20. Opportunity to take stock.

21. Help facilities.

22. Ease of repetition.

23. Ease of short-cutting.

24. Adequacy of internal instructions.

25. Adequacy of documentation.

26. Adequacy of worksheets.

27. Adequacy of follow-up instructions.

28. Accuracy of content.

29. Order of content.

30. Completeness of content.

31. Ideas for teacher modification.

Overall response to the program of the;

32. Best pupils.

33. Average pupils.

34. Worst pupils.

Overall response of other teachers;

35. With expertise in subject area.

36. Without expertise in subject area.

Overall response of other teachers;

37. Sympathetic to CAL programs.

38. Unsympathetic to CAL programs.

You will notice that the list contains many similar items to those suggested for software selection, so if you have already read chapter four, most categories will need little introduction nor indeed explanation. The important thing to bear in mind is that instruments of this kind are intended for use after acquiring some experience of using the program in the classroom, presumably after having undertaken the software selection process itself.

QUALITATIVE APPROACHES

Unlike the quantitative approaches discussed previously, the essence of the qualitative approach is to provide a much fuller picture of how the software is actually used, and the users' reactions towards it. For this reason, evidence is very often descriptive, or even anecdotal, and can be the result of in-depth observation of, or discussion with a small number of subjects over a relatively long period of time. It is just as legitimate to obtain evidence from the pupils as it is from the teacher, but in addition the observations of an independent observer who watches and records the activities of teacher and pupils together can provide valuable insights into a program's effectiveness.

COLLECTING DATA

There are many ways in which qualitative data can be collected and used to help evaluate the effectiveness of computer programs. It is always best, if at all possible, to aim for evidence using at least two different methods so that information can be compared for similarities and/or differences. Remember that your conclusions can be reached with a far greater degree of certainty if they can be supported by several pieces of different evidence. In such a case we normally say that the evidence is 'triangulated'. Among the many different approaches available to the teacher undertaking such small-scale observation or research are:

1. Field-notes,

2. Case studies,

3. Diaries kept by pupils or the teacher,

4. Interviews and discussions,

5. Video recordings.

KEEPING FIELD-NOTES

Keeping your own field notes is a very good way of recording observations, reflections and reactions to a variety of classroom issues, not just those concerned specifically with the evaluation of educational software. Many teachers make such observations in a book as a regular and ongoing part of their own personal and professional development. Usualy, the best way to go about writing field-notes is to jot down thoughts,

113

feelings and observations as the lesson is in progress. However, this is not always the most practical thing to do and so immediately after the lesson may be more appropriate sometimes. Whatever you choose to do, it is important to elaborate on the original notes as soon after the lesson as you can, while the events of the lesson and your awareness of your original thinking are still clear in your mind.

There are three major ways in which field notes might be used as an aid to evaluating software in the classroom;

a. they can focus on a particular issue over a period of time. Things like time spent on or off task while sitting at the computer, or the ability of a program to encourage cooperation, discussion and teamwork when a small group of children are working on a problem together,

b. they can reflect general impressions of the classroom and its climate, thus providing a comparison between times when children are using the program, and times when they are not,

c. they can provide an ongoing description of an individual child or group of children as they interact with the program. This kind of data is particularly useful if a case-study is being constructed.

In every case the teacher can be collecting information by simply observing the children from afar, by listening in to childrens' conversations or by asking questions and discussing ideas.

Hopkins (1985), suggests that the major advantages of field notes are;

a. they are so simple to keep and no outside help is needed, ideal for the teacher working alone,

b. they provide a good on-going record,

c. the information so gathered can be easily studied in the teacher's own time,

d. they can serve as an aide-memoire,

e. they can help to relate incidents and to explore emerging trends,

f. they provide valuable material for case-studies.

However the disadvantages are,

1. they need to fall back on aids such as question-analysis sheets, tapes and transcripts for specific information,

2. that actual conversations are virtually impossible to record by field notes,

3. a notebook works well with a small group but not so well with a full class,

4. they are initially rather time-consuming until you get into the swing of things,

5. they are highly subjective.

Field-notes can be an important and integral part of a teacher's collection of information in preparation for writing a report or evaluation of a particular program in the classroom. To this can be added examples of the children's work and even accounts of the children's own reactions to the program. Mick Nadal undertook one such evaluation of 'Micro-Map' (Ladybird-Longman, 1985) with his own class in College House Junior school, Chilwell, Nottingham. (At the time of writing this was expected to be published as one of the MEP 'Classroom Reports'. See Blunt, 1985). In fact, what Nadal did was more than just an evaluation of a single program. What he set out to do was to;

...use the computer as a medium to gain an integrated curriculum that fulfils the criteria of our school's educational aims and objectives, and at the same time has a context that is constant throughout.

His starting point was taken from a topic on mazes, which the children had been working on previously. Looking at 'things similar to mazes', street plans and maps led conveniently into the use of the 'Micro-Map' program. As Nadal describes in his own words;

The program is basically skills learning and practice which involves skills associated with mapping, such as co-ordinates, points of the compass, scale and distance. For the purposes of these exercises there are maps of an imaginary area supplied. Also in with the package there are a number of information and work sheets.

Working with the program itself the children were able to explore many of the features on the map supplied which led to

115

work away from the computer. This included such things as
co-ordinates, scale and distance and reading the features and
terrain on other maps. The map-based work also led a variety
of other creative activities including the exploration of a
local census, a local radio news program, a local newspaper and
local council elections. Furthermore, these activities were
enhanced by the addition of a number of other computer
programs, including extensive use of a word processor.

Work on each of the features of the map in the program was
varied and stimulating. What follows is an example of what
Nadal says about just one of them; the Old Mill;

> A class lesson debated the use of the mill. Eventually a
> vote decided that it should be a craft shop and studio.
> Next the residents were arranged. Charles Brown was to be
> a wood carver and his wife Sylvia to be a potter.
> From this start the children added ages, and a family.
> They then wrote individual stories about the family. With
> the aid of a very good calendar picture of a mill, plus
> some technical information formed into a text on the word
> processor, a customised poster for the Old
> Mill - Ferndale, was prepared.
> Two girls in the class go to pottery lessons on Saturday
> mornings, and with the aid of their really delightful
> pieces, "Sylvia Brown" mounted an exhibition. Posters,
> signs and handbills were prepared by the children and
> myself, and other classes invited to come and see the
> work. This was later developed by the visit of a friend
> of mine who is a carver. She did some clay carvings with
> some of the children, who produced some very attractive
> carved and slip painted tiles which she then took to a
> pottery for firing. At the same time the children used
> slip to draw pictures or used leaves as templates to help
> them decorate some unfired pots. My friend had been given
> these and some clay by the pottery and while they were at
> it, the children also made some coil pots and small
> animals, which also went for glazing and firing. So we
> had the makings of "Sylvia Brown's" second exhibition, but
> this time produced in school.

Using this, and other activities, Nadal was able to draw upon
aspects of a wide range of the school curriculum. Mathematics,
language skills, creative language, geography, history, science
and craft, design and technology were all integrated into the
topic.

In his discussion of the work, Nadal notes that, with such
a wide-ranging project;

> ...the preparation of information and worksheets is very
> time consuming and for the children to maintain a high
> level of enthusiasm for two whole terms, the different

aspects of the topic needed to be handled in as many different ways as possible.

This illustrates an important point about the use of computer programs in the classroom, being a good example of how a program or programs are used to stimulate, maintain or reinforce classroom activities, but never constituting the whole activity. Nadal goes on to comment that:

However, the whole idea of creating an imaginary community was a very stimulating exercise for me, and I was therefore able to pass this on to the class. Also the linking together of the subjects, using the theme of a village, has created a fuller context for the work to take place in.

Comments of this kind give us a valuable clue as to the effectiveness of 'Micro-map' and, to a lesser extent, the other programs used in the topic. An important feature of effective teaching is for the teacher to convey enthusiasm and a sense of relevance to the children. Of course another, and extremely valuable, clue to the effectiveness of the project can be found in the teacher's comments about the quality of the children's work. Nadal comments:

Both the quantity and the quality of the work that the children produced showed a marked improvement during the course of the two terms. These improvements of course, may have been possible to achieve working in another way. Certain aspects, however, appear to have benefitted noticeably from the approach used. In working on a topic involving the whole class and contributed to by them, their attitude to each other has been the best that I have ever encountered in a class.

Of course, this account refers to more than just the effects of using the computer program, and so it is not easy to attribute any one of the benefits to any particular activity, teaching method or resource used. Nevertheless, it does make a very clear suggestion as to an effective way of using the program in question. After all if, as I have suggested, we are to consider computer programs simply as one resource among many, their effectiveness can only be properly evaluated when seen in use within that context.

USING A DETACHED OBSERVER

In recent years the trend has been for the act of teaching to become a more open and public affair. By this I mean that as

117

attitudes towards the curriculum have changed, teachers have tended to work together more often in teams. Also, as the internal geography of schools has changed, it has become increasingly necessary for teachers and children to adapt to working within the sight and sound of others. As a result of this, many more teachers are happy to work in the presence of other teachers, and pupils of all ages are quite used to other teachers, or even relative strangers being around while they are working. For this reason it is probably easier to make use of a colleague as a detached observer in the classroom than ever before. However, it would be wrong to assume that the presence of an observer would have no effect upon the performance and behaviour of the teacher or the children, and so care must be taken to minimise such 'observer effects'. (See Blease, 1983, for a fuller account of this effect).

The major advantage of using a detached observer is that it frees the teacher from having to act as classroom manager, teacher and adviser, as well as classroom researcher. Of course there are disadvantages too, since there is always the possibility that the observer may misinterpret what is observed unless ample provision is made for discussion between teacher and observer both before and after the lesson. Observations can be as structured or as informal as you like. The observer can be given a list of particular items of behaviour to look out for, simply recording when and how often they occur, where they occur and by whom. Alternatively, the observer may make a descriptive written record of the way a group interacts with the program and each other. This can include details of the strategies adopted in much more depth than normally available to the teacher alone. Taking a wider perspective, the observer could observe, record and reflect upon the use of the computer or a specific program in the context of the whole class activity, or even the whole school. This could include consideration of the teacher's own effectiveness, interaction with the computer group, and the extent to which the program had actually liberated the teacher to work with other children uninterrupted.

Malcolm Lewis acted as an independent observer for Adrian Jackson of Hengrove school in Bristol, who was using 'Tray' with a sixth form 'A' level English group. (See Blunt, 1984, 'Tray for Modern Languages and 6th Form Poetry'). The details of this program were introduced earlier in this chapter, so I will not repeat them. However it is worth noting the contrast between the approaches taken by the two teachers involved since, in the first case the pupils' reactions were elicited using a checklist or questionnaire, and in the following example an observer was used to take a more detached, but less structured view.

Jackson's first objective was to see whether a program like 'Tray' had a place at this level of literature study. Even the choice of text to be used was made after considerable discussion between teacher and observer, finally settling on Norman MacCraig's poem 'Frustrated Virtuoso'. As this was a poem, Jackson felt that it was important to indicate the positions of the ends of the lines, this he did by adding asterisks as if they were part of the regular punctuation of the poem. It was at this point that opinions differed since Lewis, the observer, felt that;

> ...signalling line endings from the start in this way pre-empts a benefit of exploring poems via 'Tray'. It may sound paradoxical, but the uncertainty about line arrangements, as the process of revelation gets under way, actually draws attention to the visual layout of the lines - sometimes very important in appreciating a poem's overall form,...(p.32)

It was not possible to discount the novelty effect of using the computer for the two groups observed since it was the first time that they had attempted such an exercise. As Lewis comments:

> There is no doubt that their sustained concentration on the program was initially largely due to the novelty of the machine and the enjoyment of the game qualities of the program. My presence as an outsider also contributed to the extra-ordinariness of the occasion.(p.32)

However, after describing the students' initial reactions to the program and the hidden text, Lewis's attention turns to higher level learning activities which give us a clearer idea of the possibilities of a program like 'Tray' for 6th form work:

> After a while, however, the possibilities in this somewhat mechanical process become exhausted. Sufficient textual information is on the screen to encourage the exercise of intellectual skills of a rather higher order. The 'developing' text itself becomes much more important and is the object of quite intensive interrogation by students. Here, the collaboration possible in the attack of many members of a small group really comes into its own. The dumb quality of the computer seems to prompt unrestrained airing of ideas, questions, guesses, counter-suggestions, and decision-making within the group.(p.32)

The observer's description of the events of the lesson also threw light upon individual characteristics and strengths of members within the group, something which is of great potential value to the teacher:

> Listening to the groups' discussions as they worked one
> can be in little doubt that a range of skills and reading
> strategies are in play....The quality of discussion and
> interrogation of the text, and of the creative thinking it
> evidenced, was impressive. There was a particularly sharp
> girl in one group, whose speculations about unrevealed
> portions of the poem were almost extraordinarily and
> consistently accurate.
> Fortunately her sense of deference to others in the group,
> and to the group as a whole, was also highly advanced:
> although prominent, she was not arrogant or coercive in
> the way she proposed ideas, and was often challenged by
> others and gave way to them without difficulty. (p.33)

However, evidence of this kind does more than just tell us
about individual characteristics, since it clearly indicates
the quality of thinking, and the level of social and
intellectual skills demanded by the program.

KEEPING A DIARY

A useful variation on making field notes is to write up one's
observations each lesson in the form of a diary. Over the
period of a topic, a term or a year this can accumulate a great
deal of valuable information about both resources and pupils.
When evaluating a computer program it might be sufficient to
make entries in the diary only on those occasions when the
program is actually being used. On the other hand our
discussion of the evaluation of 'Micro-Map' by Nadal might
suggest that entries should be made after all lessons since it
will give a better view of the program within the context of
the whole curriculum. It is quite likely that some of the
effects of a good program may transfer into other aspects of
the school day.
   Pupil diaries can also function as valuable sources of
feedback to the teacher about the effectiveness of a computer
program and of teaching in general. They can also provide a
valuable and convenient source of contrast and cross-reference
to the teacher's own diary entries or field notes. Hopkins
(1985), suggests three uses of pupil diaries in this context;

they provide a pupil perspective on a teaching episode,

they provide data on the general climate of the classroom,

they provide information for triangulation.(p.64)

120

Stewart (1985), attempted to assess the effectiveness of Logo
and turtles with 6-7 year old children in a Devon infant school
by observing groups of selected children on five occasions at
weekly intervals. In order to show change and development in
the thinking behind the actions made, and decisions taken by
the children over that five week period, Stewart wrote up her
notes in diary form. Although Stewart was not the children's
regular teacher, there is no reason why she could not have
been. Since observations were not made all day, every day, the
regular teacher could have set aside some time once a week to
make reasonably detailed observations of children using the
computer without upsetting the normal classroom routine.
Additional, less detailed diary entries could then have been
made at other times during the week.

Week 1

After talking about safety precautions, the children were shown
how to operate the turtle in the immediate mode, i.e. every
command entered is executed immediately the RETURN key is
pressed.
The children then experimented with estimation of distances
and, with Stewart's help, worked out how to make the turtle
draw a square. In this first session Stewart notes some
difficulty with the notation of three-digit numbers, e.g. 205
instead of 250, and a certain amount of confusion over the
concepts of left and right.

Week 2

Stewart set the children a problem which involved guiding the
turtle through a maze, still in the immediate mode. It soon
became evident that, in such a problem-solving situation, the
children worked independently rather that cooperatively. The
exercise provided additional practice in estimation skills and
introduced the need to record what they had done. The
difficulty with forward and rotational moves was seen to
persist.

Week 3

Stewart introduced the idea of entering instructions as a
procedure. She noted much confusion here because the turtle no
longer operated in the immediate mode. This provides a good
example of how keeping a record of events can highlight points
of particular difficulty with a computer program. This is
further exemplified by the persistent problem of the separation
of forward and rotational moves for the third consecutive week.
At this point one might normally expect the teacher to provide
additional help with such a difficulty. This does not appear
to have happened, but if Stewart had been the children's

regular teacher, one might reasonably expect that she would have done.

Week 4

Stewart attempted to consolidate the process of procedure-writing by presenting the groups with a new maze. It was at this point that individual approaches to solving this problem arose. One boy in particular, revealed a particular talent for applying his previous experience with Big Trak (a computerised toy) to the solution of the maze problem. Other children attempted to de-bug their procedures by forming and testing hypotheses.

Week 5

In this session some of the children explored the drawing of a triangle, showing some facility with the 'total trip theorem', i.e. the drawing of an enclosed shape involves the turtle rotating through 360 degrees, to calculate exterior angles. This sounds like a large step from the previous work, but in fact some of the children were involved in carol singing practice and so the groups were smaller and could benefit from more teacher help.

In conclusion, Stewart draws together some of the elements of the activity over the five week period, and provides us with a clue to her own feelings about the effectiveness of floor turtles in the infant classroom:

> Although the study was only carried out over a short period, progress was visible in each of the eight children observed. Over the study period the children had been using a number of important skills which included estimation, forming an hypothesis, attempting to determine cause-and-effect relationships, recording skills, sequential logical reasoning, internalizing angular measurement and developing basic programming skills. All the children enjoyed working with the turtle and, in the case of James, demonstrated ability that had lain undiscovered. Although the groups were small and a lot of attention was given to the children, it was evident that they were developing a degree of independence. Eventually the children could be expected to work without supervision for up to 30 minutes, if safety precautions were adhered to. Working with the turtle, the children were coming into contact with concepts and skills which in conventional classrooms would be difficult to teach; as such I believe that the turtle earns its place in the classroom.

USING THE CHILDREN'S PERSPECTIVES

I have suggested on several occasions that teachers can obtain useful observations on the effectiveness of computer programs by simply observing and listening to what the children say. I often feel that those who say children lack the experience and maturity to make worthwhile judgements about the product that they receive in the classroom, do many children a great injustice. In the appropriate circumstances, children of all ages are capable of making observations about the teaching they receive, observations which exhibit a great deal of insight and good sense. So far I have suggested two ways in which children's views might be elicited, firstly, using a checklist or questionnaire, and secondly, by asking them to keep a diary or log book of their experiences and feelings about the programs that they are using. Of course, an even more straightforward approach would be simply to ask them. However, you may feel that this is rather unsystematic, providing no more than the most elementary of feedback.

Another way in which the children's reactions to the software can be determined is to organise its use in such a way that a group of children are responsible for agreeing upon, and writing up, a report on the work undertaken. This is a good way of dealing with a content-free tool like a data-base since it offers the opportunity to describe in detail how the program was actually used, the kinds of advantages that it brought to the work, and the users' reactions towards it. With utility programs of this kind this is far preferable to a series of ticks and crosses on a checklist. This was the approach taken by the teacher of class 5R of Fox Primary school in London.(Primary Contact, 1985). The children undertook to write an account of their use of the microcomputer in helping analyse the findings of a fossil 'dig' using a graphics/data-handling package called 'Dataprobe' (Addison Wesley). This is how the children described their first visit to the quarry:

...A hundred years ago, some people wanted chalk to make chemicals. They dug chalk from the quarries. One quarry was at Pebblecombe on the North Downs, twenty miles south of school. Then they stopped using the quarry. It became overgrown with weeds and plants.
The quarry was deserted, with its fossils in it, until classes 5R and 5M went there to find fossils in September 1984. We wanted to dig out the fossils of the shells that had died millions of years earlier, caught in the chalk rocks.
The quarry was enormous. There were cliffs about 40 feet high. We could see the layers of chalk running

across the quarry. In front of us was a great slope of broken chalk rocks that led up to the cliff face. (p.117)

After spending a whole day there, scrambling over the rocks, collecting specimens and inspecting the various strata, they wrote:

We dug nearly a whole day, and brought back 97 rocks to display. I found one. There are probably millions more just waiting to be found at Pebblecombe quarry.

Of course, just collecting rocks in an unsystematic way provides little evidence of how the various finds relate to the strata in the quarry, and so the children had devised a simple way to record where specimens were found and who found them:

We only tapped the rock lightly, then it would crack open. If you found a fossil in it, you had to put the fossils in a bag, with a piece of paper. On the paper we wrote our names and where we found the fossil. (p.117)

Once back in school the children set about describing and identifying as many of the fossils as possible, each specimen being given an identification number. This was the start of collating the many items of information about each one. Then they started to formulate questions about the location of their finds:

We wondered where most of the fossils were found. Most of them seemed to be from the bottom, because this was where it was easiest to look for them.
    Only a few of the fossils were found on the top slope. There was less space up here, and not so many broken rocks. Also the chalk face was very narrow, just under the grass at the top. (p.118)

These comments give us some idea about the children's ability to consider the reliability of their data, they seem to be aware of the problems of non-random sampling, although not in so many words. Of course, what we do not know is how much help they received from their teacher. Nevertheless, one way or the other, it is an important information-handling skill to have mastered.
    The sorting of the data was to be done using the computer, and so the children set about entering as much information as they could about each fossil onto coding sheets containing eleven fields, i.e. eleven separate pieces of information about each fossil.

Here are the chosen fields:

1. Number of rock
2. Name of fossil
3. Length of fossil (cms) with a decimal point
4. Width of fossil (cms) with a decimal point
5. Was the fossil found on the rock face or loose?
6. Name of finder
7. East coordinate for location of fossil
8. North coordinate for location of fossil
9. Class of finder (5M or 5R)
10. Was it an actual fossil or an impression?
11. Was the fossil whole or only a part?

These were then typed into the data-base making 148 records, one for each fossil. Setting up the data-base in this way clearly enabled the children to investigate their data in ways which would normally have been unheard of given the time available. This, in itself, provides us and the teacher with ample evidence for the effectiveness of the program, something which is confirmed by the mature and enthusiastic way in which the children describe their activities:

> We then used the computer to sort out all the fossils as we wanted. Sometimes we had them all put on a list...We could show the fossil names on a piechart, too.
> We could get the computer to draw a picture of the quarry (previously prepared by the teacher), and put on it a little mark where each of the fossils we were interested in were found. (p.119)

The children also competently employed histograms, scatter graphs and Venn diagrams, all constructed by the computer program, to explore their hypotheses about the fossils they had found.

As a record of the children's work, the report with its associated charts, diagrams, graphs and drawings provided the children with a superb medium through which to illustrate and display the fruits of their obvious enthusiasm and hard work. However, this also provides for the teacher, and any other interested reader, a great deal of evidence as to the effectiveness of the computer program used. Since the data-base/graphics package formed such a central and integral part of the work, and little of the analysis would have been possible without it; the quality of the work speaks for itself.

In this example, the children were not specifically asked to write about their experiences with the computer, it just happened that the program formed an important part of the whole project. Of course in some ways that is just how it should be, since computer programs are seldom ends in themselves. There is no reason, however, why a teacher should not ask for a more specific account of experiences using a computer program. Alternatively, one possible approach which is an interesting and useful exercise for the participants themselves is for the report to take the form of a guide for future users, to help them tackle the program more quickly and efficiently.

USING INTERVIEWS AND DISCUSSIONS

There are several ways in which interviews or discussions may be used to obtain information about the effectiveness of a computer program. The four most common are:

1. The teacher interviews individual pupils about their experiences using the program and tries to find out what the pupils think they have learned or achieved by its use.

2. A detached observer, usually another teacher in the school, interviews individual pupils. In addition to their views about the program, the interviewer can try to find out their views on how effectively their teacher used it.

3. Pupils can be encouraged to interview other pupils who have used the program. These can be most productive because the interviewee is less likely to feel the constraints of talking to an adult authority figure. If the interviewer is well briefed by the teacher, and has an interview schedule, a great deal of information can be elicited. One student of mine has had considerable success with this technique, even with children in her infant class.

4. The teacher can be interviewed by a detached observer who has watched how the program has been used in the class for some time. This is an important extension of having an independent observer in the classroom, providing the opportunity for teacher and observer to agree on the most appropriate interpretation of the behaviour observed. It is very important for the observer to understand what was going on in the lesson as it was understood by the participants themselves. Classroom behaviour is only meaningful if the observer has knowledge of what was in the minds of the observed. In this way the observer can come to understand why they acted in that way. Clearly it is important to understand the teacher's objectives in any lesson before any assessment can be made as to its effectiveness. Therefore it follows that the observer needs to know what the teacher expected to achieve with

a computer program before its effectiveness can be assessed in that context.

However, interviewing is not something which you can do without adequate preparation. I have already suggested that the pupil-interviewer needs to be provided with an appropriate interview schedule, but of course this is also true for other interviewers as well. The results of your interviews will only be comparable if you ask the same questions throughout. Before you start you must think carefully what it is that you want to know. Keep your questions as simple and straightforward as possible, make sure that they are appropriate to the abilities and experience of your interviewees, and arrange them into some sort of logical order. If you have avoided more open-ended questions, try to provide time at the end of the interview for them to express any views or ideas which were not covered by your schedule.

Your actual interviewing technique is important too. This is what Walker and Adelman (1975), have to say about that;

1. be a sympathetic, interested and attentive listener, without taking an active conservative role; this is a way of conveying that you value and appreciate the child's opinion,

2. be neutral with respect to subject matter. Do not express your own opinions either on the subjects being discussed by the children or on the children's ideas about these subjects, and be especially careful not to betray feelings of surprise or disapproval at what the child knows,

3. your own sense of ease is also important. If you feel hesitant or hurried, the students will sense this feeling and behave accordingly,

4. the students may also be fearful that they will expose an attitude or idea that you don't think is correct. Reassure along the lines of 'Your opinions are important to me. All I want to know is what you think - this isn't a test and there isn't any one answer to the questions I want to ask',

5. specifically we suggest that you:
   *phrase questions similarly each time
   *keep the outline of interview questions before you
   *be prepared to reword a question if it is not understood or if the answer is vague and too general. Sometimes it is hard not to give an 'answer' to the question in the process of rewording it. (p.140)

127

There will be many occasions when a formal interview is just not appropriate. Time may be short, or you may not want to disturb the normal classroom routine. In these circumstances, you may feel that a less formal group, or class discussion is more suitable. However, it is still important to know what it is that you want to find out. Your preparation for this discussion must be as detailed as for the interview, but your method of organisation and presentation will be different, and must appear to be more spontaneous to the pupils concerned. In the case of your interviews, it would probably be a good idea to use a tape recorder so that you do not appear to be constantly writing notes. In an informal discussion however, this could prove to be somewhat inhibiting for the pupils, and so you might need to retain more of the information in your head to be written down later on. If you do take notes during an interview or discussion, it is good technique not to be seen writing vigorously after someone has just said something which is controversial. Keep it at the back of your mind and write it down when the conversation has returned to a more neutral subject.

MAKING VIDEO RECORDINGS

While it is still true that video cameras are relatively few and far between in schools, particularly in small ones, they are beginning to appear. Very many schools own at least one video recorder which is used for off-air recordings of those schools broadcasts which are free from copyright restrictions. The next step, as and when the money becomes available, is often to buy a camera which can be used to record school events, drama sessions, and perhaps provide the means whereby some students can explore the world of film and television production. Even if your school does not have these facilities yet, it is worthwhile considering for a moment what might be possible in the future.

A video recorder allows the teacher to observe many aspects of classroom life without having to rely upon the good nature of their colleagues to observe, make notes and comment upon what they see and hear. The information which it provides is both accurate and heuristic. The whole recording can be viewed over and over again at leisure, providing the opportunity for the teacher to concentrate upon different aspects of the lesson at different times. Of course, the pupils need time to get used to having the equipment around, but this is easily accomplished by providing time for them to see and perhaps use it themselves on several occasions before the real recordings are made. This is an approach which I have found most effective when using a radio microphone in the classroom. It is not long before most pupils lose interest. If the camera is set up on a tripod overlooking the computer area, it is possible to keep track of all movements around it while the program is in use. The microphone can be strategically positioned to pick up all conversation in the area, and if it is also possible to see what appears on the screen, all the better. While recording is taking place it is always better to make sure that the monitor is turned off so that it does not distract the pupils from their work.

Hopkins (1985), suggests three uses of video recorders in classroom research, each of which applies equally well to the collection of information for software evaluation;

*in obtaining visual material of the total teaching situation,

*in acting as an aid to diagnosis,

*as a means of examining in detail a specific teaching episode. (p.71)

Of course, alongside the obvious advantages of using a video recorder, there are some disadvantages which must be taken into account. The equipment is still very expensive to obtain. However, as with all things electronic, the price is bound to come down as manufacturers recoup their extensive development costs. As more self-contained camera-recorders become available, i.e. those which house the cassette inside the camera instead of in a separate recorder, the equipment will become less bulky, and therefore easier to use. It is also true that camera equipment can be conspicuous and distracting, but as I have already suggested, this can be overcome by careful preparation. Finally, however, there is one problem which is more difficult to overcome, although it is not confined to video recording alone. What finally appears on the tape for analysis is very much the product of whoever was directing the camera at the time of recording. If the teacher sets up the camera on a tripod, then it is the teacher who has defined the limits of the field of view. If a colleague or pupil is given the task of operating the camera, the result will be a statement of how that operator saw the situation at the time. In other words, the operator acts as an editor. As I have suggested on previous occasions, it is important for the teacher to have a clear idea in mind of what is required. If the act of software evaluation is to be shared with a colleague, it is important that both parties agree on what they are looking for. Pupils who are to be given the task of operating the equipment must be adequately briefed.

A BRIEF NOTE ON INTERPRETATION

It does not matter which method or methods you choose to collect information about the effectiveness of a computer program in your classroom, the important question to ask is 'effective for what?' As I have emphasised on many occasions, computer programs, and all other teaching and learning resources for that matter, can only be selected or evaluated in terms of the objectives that the teacher has in mind for them. All selection and evaluation must be an attempt to assess whether the resource will be, or has been effective in achieving the teacher's objectives for the group or class of pupils involved. This means that the same program may be judged more effective with one class than another, or for one set of objectives than another.

ADAPTING TO THE MICRO

There is no question about it, the microcomputer is not going to take over from the teacher. Instead, if properly used, it will increasingly become a powerful and versatile resource in the classroom. For this to happen, it is important for teachers to adapt in such a way that they can ensure its maximum positive effect. In the worlds of work and leisure the computer is here to stay, and it is only right and natural that this should be adequately reflected in our schools. Children need to acquire the ability to discriminate between abuse and the good use of microtechnology. There is no better place to start than in school, learning from the good example of their teachers. I would suggest that there are three things to aim for if this is to become a reality:

1. become fully familiar with the strengths and weaknesses of the microcomputer as a teaching and learning resource,

2. through practice, ensure that informed software selection and evaluation become second nature to you,

3. only use the computer when you are sure that it is appropriate to do so. Be ready to justify its use in terms of its advantages over other methods and media, and your own particular objectives for that lesson.

APPENDIX

A SUMMARY OF SOFTWARE SELECTION CRITERIA

1. DOCUMENTATION: (i) Technical

    a. Does the program have any accompanying documentation? p.74

    b. Are there any simple loading and running instructions? p.74

    c. Does the program require anything other than the most elementary knowledge of the computer to get it up and running? p.74

    d. Are hardware requirements made explicit in the simplest of terms? p.75

    e. Are instructions given for making a back-up copy of the tape or disc? If not, do the publishers offer a replacement service for corrupted discs and tapes? p.76

    f. Does the documentation include a list of other machines for which a version of the program is available? p.76

DOCUMENTATION: (ii) Information about the program

    a. Are the aims and objectives of the program made clear? p.76

    b. Does it specify the age and ability range for which it was designed? What degree of flexibility does it provide? p.77

    c. What kind of program is it? p.77

d. Does the program allow for any alterations to be made? If so, are the instructions unambiguous and easy for the non-expert to follow? p.78

e. Does the documentation contain instructions for a 'browse mode' or details of a 'sample run'? p.78

2. PRESENTATION AND LAYOUT

Text

a. Are instructions clear and unambiguous? p.79

b. Is each frame attractively presented avoiding irrelevant detail? p.81

c. Have coloured and double height characters been used to their best advantage? p.81

Graphics

d. Is the use of graphics appropriate to the aims and objectives of the program? p.81

e. If pictures and diagrams are included, could they be represented more effectively by some other means? eg. a printed sheet, a map or a photograph. p.82

Sound

f. If sound effects are included, do they constitute an essential and integral part of the program? p.83

g. Does the program provide a simple means whereby the volume can be controlled or the sound can be turned off completely? p.83

3. FRIENDLINESS AND FLEXIBILITY

a. Does the program provide helpful messages to correct errors? p.84

b. Is sufficient help provided so that pupils can understand the program without your constant intervention? p.85

c. Is the program sufficiently versatile so that the user can control what it does? p.85

   d. Is the program sufficiently flexible to be applicable
      in a variety of teaching/learning situations? p.85

4. ACHIEVEMENT OF STATED AIMS

   a. Without actually using the program, and keeping your
      own pupils in mind, to what extent do you think the
      program would achieve its/your aims and objectives?
      p.85

5. ROBUSTNESS

   a. Is it easy for the user to correct typing errors? p.86

   b. Are possible errors trapped? When numerical input is
      required, what happens if you type in a word? What
      happens if you type in a number when a word is
      required? p.87

   c. When textual input is required, what is the longest
      sentence you can input? Does the program crash if you
      enter a longer one? p.87

   d. Can you get all the way through the program without
      entering anything, just pressing the RETURN key each
      time a word, number or sentence is required? p.87

   e. When numerical input is required, what happens if you
      type in very large or very small numbers? p.87

   f. Can the program cope with an input of zero or a
      negative number? p.87

   g. Are all non-essential keys automatically turned off by
      the program itself? Try pressing some wrong keys, e.g.
      ESCAPE, BREAK, SHIFT/BREAK, the CONTROL key in
      conjunction with any others. p.88

SPECIFIC SELECTION CRITERIA

(i) Tutorial and drill and practice programs

   a. Is the content fully described? p.88

   b. Is the content of the program appropriate to the
      designer's stated aims and objectives? p.88

c. Is the content and presentation appropriate to your class and the use you have in mind? p.88

d. Is the micro appropriate for teaching this topic? p.88

e. Is the content/information accurate? p.89

f. Is the content/information accurate enough for the use you have in mind? p.89

g. Does the input format suit your purposes? Are there options from which you can choose? p.89

h. Does the program provide immediate and appropriate feedback to the user? p.89

i. Does the program keep a score or a record of the learner's progress? p.90

j. Does the program suggest pencil and paper tasks, or other work that might be carried out away from the computer? p.90

For Tutorial programs in particular

k. Is the content broken down into appropriately small and logical stages? p.90

l. Does the program allow the user to revise previous pages or follow remedial loops? p.90

m. Will the program take free-format answers in an acceptable number of forms? p.90

For drill and practice programs in particular

n. Does the program provide a variety of levels of difficulty? p.91

o. Are the examples or exercises randomly generated? p.91

(ii) Arcade-type games

a. Are the instructions clear and always available? p.91

b. Does the program provide a sufficient range of levels of difficulty and speed? p.91

c. Is the content of the program available for inspection and/or change? p.91

d. Is the content accurate? p.91

e. Does the program provide appropriate feedback to the player? p.91

f. Does the program keep a score or a record of the player's progress? p.91

g. Is the visual display likely to be attractive, exciting and absorbing? p.92

(iii) Simulation games

a. Is it appropriate to use the computer for this topic? p.92

b. Is the content of the program appropriate to your aims and to the group you have in mind? p.92

c. Are commands and instructions available throughout the program run? p.92

d. Does the program (or the documentation) give sufficient and appropriate clues if the user gets stuck? p.92

e. Is the nature of the model made explicit? p.92

f. Is there provision to change data if appropriate? p.92

g. Can a game be 'saved' and resumed later? p.92

h. Does the program give any suggestions as to how it might relate to events in the real world? p.92

(iv) Laboratory simulations

a. Is the nature of the mathematical model made specific? p.93

b. Is the range and degree of accuracy of the model discussed in the documentation? p.93

c. Is there provision for changing the data? p.93

d. Could this topic be covered more effectively with real practical work? p.93

(v) Content-free tools

Data-bases

When creating files

a. Are the instructions clear and easy to follow? p.93

b. What is the maximum number of records and fields? p.93

c. What is the maximum field size? p.94

d. Is there an option to edit and delete records? p.94

e. Can the number of records be increased after the file has been created? p.94

When interrogating files

f. Are the instructions for formulating a query clear and unambiguous? p.94

g. Is there a 'help' option to explain the commands and to describe the fields? p.94

h. Does the search option allow you to formulate both simple and complex queries? p.94

i. What is the longest query acceptable? p.94

Annan, N. (1977) Report of the Committee on the Future of Broadcasting, HMSO, London

Barnes, D. (1982) Practical Curriculum Study, Routledge and Kegan Paul, London

Bates, T. (1981) 'Towards a Better Research Framework for Evaluating the Effectiveness of Educational Media', British Journal of Educational Technology, vol.12, no.3, pp.215-233

Blake, R.M. (1984) Microcomputer Software Evaluation: The validation of a Software Acceptability Rating Scale Unpublished M.Ed. dissertation, University of Manchester.

Blease, D. (1983) 'Observer Effects on Teachers and Pupils in Classroom Research',Educational Review, vol.35, no.3, pp.213-217

Bloom, B.S. et al (1956) Taxonomy of Educational Objectives, Handbook 1:Cognitive Domain, David McKay (reprinted Longman, 1972), New York and London

Blunt, L. (ed.) (1984) MEP Classroom Reports 'Tray for Modern Languages', Published by MEP, Southbank, Mid Warwickshire College of Further Education, Warwick New Road, Leamington Spa.

Brown, I. (1984) 'Looking for Quality in Software', Educational Computing, January.

Bruner, J.S. (1966) Towards a theory of Instruction, Harvard University Press, Cambridge, Mass.

Burkhardt, H., Fraser, R. and Wells, C. (1982) 'Teaching Style and Program Design', Computers and Education, vol.6, pp.77-84

Chambers, J.A. and Sprecher, J.W. (1983) Computer Assisted Instruction. Its Use in the Classroom, Prentice Hall

Chandler, D. (1984) Young Learners and the Microcomputer, Open University Press, Milton Keynes

Croft, G. and Evans, S. (1985) 'Educational Software Review Project', Computer Education, February

Deeson, E. (1983) 'The Assessment of Learning Programs', Computers in Schools, vol.5, no.4, July, p.117

Eisner, E.W. (1969) 'Instructional and Expressive Educational Objectives:Their Formulation and Use in Curriculum' in W.J. Popham et al., Instructional Objectives, Rand McNally, Chicago

Elithorn, A. (1982) 'User Friendliness', Computers in Schools, vol.4, pt.4, July, pp.11-14

Ennever, L. and Harlen, W. (1972) With Objectives in mind, Macdonald Educational, London

Fiddy, P. (1981) 'More Professional Software is Needed', Educational Computing, June, pp.41-42

Fisher, J. (1983) 'Microcomputers in Junior Education', Junior Education, August

Gagne, R.M. (1970) The Conditions of Learning, 2nd edn., Holt, Rinehart and Winston, New York

Gagne, R.M. (1974) Essentials of Learning for Instruction, The Dryden Press, Holt, Rinehart and Winston, New York

Gagne, R.M. and Briggs, L.J. (1974) Principles of Instructional Design, Holt, Rinehart and Winston, New York

Gray, T. (1984) 'Versatile Focus', Times Educational Supplement November 19th, pp.51-52

Gray, T, and Billson, C. (1985) 'Making "Micro Map"- a case study of the development of a software package.', Primary Contact, Special issue no.3, pp.154-158

Hopkins, D. (1985) A Teacher's Guide to Classroom Research, Open University Press

Hoyle, E. (1972) 'Facing the Difficulties', Unit 13, Open University Second Level Course: The Curriculum: Context, Design and Development (Problems of Curriculum Innovation I, Units 13-15) Bletchley: The Open University

Jones, A. and Preece, J. (1984) 'Training Teachers to Assess Computer Software', Computer Education, November, pp.17-20

Kelly, A.V. (1984) Microcomputers and the Curriculum, Harper and Row, London

Kemmis, S., Atkin, R. and Wright, E. (1977) How do Students Learn?-Working Papers on Computer Assisted Learning. Occasional Paper no.5, Centre for Applied Research in Education, University of East Anglia

Kleinman, G., Humphrey, M. and van Buskirk (1982) 'Evaluating Educational Software', Creative Computing, vol.7, no.10, pp.84-91

Krathwohl, D.R., Bloom, B.S. and Masia, B.B. (1964) Taxonomy of Educational Objectives, Handbook 2: Affective Domain, McKay, New York (reprinted Longman, 1972)

Maddison, A. (1982) Microcomputers in The Classroom, Hodder and Stoughton, London

Malone, T. (1982) 'What Makes Computer Games Fun?' Computers in Schools, vol.4, no.4, pp.14-21

Martin, A. (1983) 'The Spirit of Logo Discerned', Microscope Logo Special, November, pp.2-6

Martin, A. (1985) Teaching and Learning with Logo, Croom Helm, London

MEP/CET (1984 onwards) MEP Classroom Reports, Obtainable from: R.E.S.O.U.R.C.E., S.Yorks and Humberside MEP Centre, Exeter Road, off Coventry Grove, Doncaster, S.Yorks.

McDonald, B., Atkin, R., Jenkins, D. and Kemmis, S. (1977) 'Evaluation of NDPCAL', British Journal of Educational Technology, vol.8, no.3

Mullan, T. (1982), Microscope, March, pp.36-37

Nash, A. and Ball, D. (1982) An Introduction to Microcomputers in Teaching, Hutchinson, London

Open University (1984) Micros in Schools: Educational Software, The Open University Press, Milton Keynes

Popper, K.R. (1959) The Logic of Scientific Discovery (revised 1968 and 1972) Hutchinson, London

Preece, J. and Jones, A. (1985) 'Training Teachers to Select Educational Computer Software: Results of a Formative Evaluation of an Open University Pack', British Journal of Educational Technology, no.1, vol.16, pp.9-20

Preece, J. and Squires, D. (1984) 'Selecting CAL Packages. Helping Teachers Recognise Quality Software', Computer Education, February, pp.20-21

Primary Contact (1985) 'Fossil "Hunting"; digging out the Information. Microcomputers and Palaeontology by the children of class 5R', Greater Manchester Primary Contact, Special Issue number 3, Didsbury School of Education, pp.117-120

Prosser, M.T. (1984) 'Towards More effective Evaluation Studies of Educational Media', British Journal of Educational Technology, January, vol.15, pt.1

Roberts, A. and Ewan, R.T.A. (1984) 'A case Study of Educational Microcomputer Use in Upper Schools', Research in Education, vol.32, November, pp.67-85

Ross, A. (1984) 'Learning why to Hypothesize: A case Study of Data Processing in a Primary School Classroom' in A.V.Kelly, Microcomputers and the Curriculum, Harper and Row, London

Rushby, N.J. (1979) An Introduction to Educational Computing, Croom Helm, London

Shayer, M. and Adey, P. (1981) Towards a Science of Science Teaching, Heinemann Educational Books, London

Spielman, B. (1981) 'Programs and Busy Teachers', Computers in Schools, vol.4, no.2

Spielman, B (1982) 'Simple Software', Educational Computing, vol.3, no.4, pp.18-19

Stenhouse, L. (1975) An Introduction To Curriculum Research and Development, Heinemann Educational Books, London

Stewart, E. (1985) 'Children and Turtles', Journal of Computer Assisted Learning, 1, pp.73-80

139

Bibliography

Straker, A. (1982) 'A Check-list For Teachers', Microscope 6
Telford, J. (1985) 'The Language for Learning',Acorn User,
    April
Tolkein, J.R.R. (1937) The Hobbit (also 1951, 1975, 1979 and
    1981) George Allen and Unwin, London
Tyler, R.W. (1949) Basic Principles of Curriculum and
    Instruction, Chicago University Press
Walker, R. and Adelman, C. (1975) A Guide to Classroom
    Observation, Methuen, London
Ward, R., Lindley, P., Rostron, A., Sewell, D. and Cubie, R.
    (1985) 'An Evaluation of the Language and Thought
    Software', Journal of Computer Assisted Learning, 1,
    pp.66-72

INDEX

Index